I0649937

note book

CONTENTS

NOTE BOOK

Initial Public Offering

A friend suggests that I should start by telling you something about this book, and I guess he's right.

So what is this book? This book is a small selection from a big stock of brief essays that I have written every day (one a day) over the course of what has come to be many years now. (Funny how remembering a standing date can make you forget the passing of the years during which you keep it.) I write and disseminate these essays on Facebook, using its little noticed "Notes" option. I also revise them there. And revise them. And revise them. And revise them. (One of the many charms of the notes function on Facebook is how it allows you to revise what you've already virtually published to your heart's content. I am put in mind of a remark a friend made about an advertisement for a Sunday brunch, which included *all the Chablis you care to enjoy:* "and then some," my friend waggishly added. My point being that the notes option on Facebook allows you to perform all the revisions you care to enjoy—and then some. (Many is the day I have mostly spent making small and large changes in the brief meditation pertaining thereto.)

I return now to the task at hand. What are these brief essays? Well probably, the easiest way to find out is to stop reading this introduction right now and go straight to the essays themselves. (After all, there is always something at least a little asinine and asymmetrical about even the most necessary introductions. At least so it has always seemed to me.)

But maybe I can and should provide a few words that might prepare you for what might otherwise seem merely strange. Let me first say a little about the form of these essays. They usually begin with a quotation, typically literary or philosophical in nature—although sometimes from some relatively recent or out-of-date biography of Eleanor Roosevelt or a handbook to Hawaiian flora and fauna or a study of Lou Kahn or a guide to Madrid or a living letter from a dead friend or something else that happens to catch my eye that day. (That said, I should say what will be apparent from even a casual glance: there are a few key texts to which these little essays, like so many homing pigeons, or callers to the heart, are forever returning. I won't burden you with listing these greatest hits, or explaining why I keep coming back to them. That, I hope, will become clear through the essays themselves.)

These quotations are followed by what I have to say, more or less directly about them. The relation between what I talk about in the essay and the text about which I am supposedly talking may not always be as explicit as those of us accustomed to the contemporary protocols of critical responsiveness are trained to expect, but they are certainly always incited by it. They are as much incited by them as a hidden god or a powerful parent or a love or a loss that touches everything we do, often most tellingly, by not saying so, and not saying how. And they are continuously informed by them, sometimes sounding them out just by sounding like them when they seem to be talking about something completely different. (It's like the time, years ago, my mother's oldest brother told me over a picnic table in a small town, north of Spokane, that I had my mother's laugh—by which he meant that I bore her whole being.)

Following the body of the essay there is usually a footnote that echoes and expands upon the writing that has preceded it. (That footnote, by the way, bears little conspicuous resemblance to a traditional explanatory or bibliographic footnote. It consists of another very brief quotation from some book or song or some something else, and its relation to the text above it is often as oblique as the relation of that text to the quotation above that.)

Finally, there is (I should say there was) a photograph: a visual correlative or collage of the sentiments verbalized in the written element of the essay. (As you will see, the essays collected in book form have been for the most part shorn of those images: here I am nearing a matter I will only mention now, and consider more fully a little later—what is lost and what is gained in the work of translation from the liquidity of the Internet to the solidity of the traditional text.)

I have arranged these notes in chronological order, largely because I couldn't think of any better way to organize them. (There are a couple of places where this won't be apparent. As you'll see, I number each note and a few times over the course of the years I've mixed up the numbering. I have a particular problem with numbers and in general everyone, sometimes, has a hard time keeping count of something over a long period of time.) In any case, as I say, these notes are arranged in chronological order. Thus, even a quick survey of what I have put together here will reveal that over the course of the last six years or so, these notes, like their author, have both changed and stayed the same. How have they stayed the same? Well, that part is pretty easy to say (though, I suspect, not always so easy to see). One way or another, with the exception of the occasional homey anecdote or homemade aphorism, most of what I have written has been a reaction to something I have read (the text set out in part or in its entirety at the beginning of the note). Here I observe the standard practice of my profession as a literary critic and my proclivity as a bookworm. (That's not so strange, right? People of all persuasions are always reacting to *something*, more or less near, more or less dear.)

How have these notes changed? That part is a little harder to describe, because there are many ways that they have changed. Let me mention just two that I think might interest you. One is quite conspicuous: Looking at what I've written over the course of many years now, I'm struck by the different styles I've used to try to address my reader: plain and fancy, direct and indirect. And it's occurred to me as I've been reviewing some of my old attempts to reach my audience (how painful to read some of them are!) that it can be as hard to sympathize with your own old selves as it is to sympathize with anyone else. Something tells me, though, that it's important to try. (I try to remember that even when I was showing myself off, I was also trying to show something beyond me.) While it sure can't stay there, sympathy has to begin somehow in your own backyard.

The second change I want to mention is a little more embedded, a little less visible at first glance. Do you remember how Don Quixote got his start, reading all those books about knight-errantry until he came to believe that he was a knight himself and set out on all those knight-errant–type errands to save those he saw in distress? Well, something like what happened to Don Quixote happened to me. (It happens to a lot of people, when you think about it.) Something like what happened to Don Quixote happened to me (though I'm not nearly so crazy and pretty far from chivalrous).

Over time, I have grown closer and closer in these notes to the texts that I take up in them: so much so that I have wound up mixing them more and more with stories from my own life—and yours (the adventures of heart and mind we share as citizens of a state of heart and mind whose messages are conveyed by social media ranging from the most well-preserved canons and commas to the bright lights and warp speeds of the Internet). As the years have passed, these notes have grown less and less formal expositions and explications of the texts where they get their start, and more and more emulations and extensions of them.

Here's an irony as old as the hills and as any story of introjection told in prose or rhyme: as these notes have become less detached from and more involved with the texts that brought them into being, the texts themselves have often disappeared from view, their influence most acute at their vanishing—like so many of the things that carry us through: like so many of the things that we carry and carry on.

All this to say that however removed they may seem from them, these are Essays in Criticism—in some familiar, though sometimes forgotten, old- and new-fashioned sense. The great ancestors of this little adventure in the essay form (Montaigne, Bacon, Johnson, De Quincey, Benjamin, Barthes, *inter alia*) always sought through their words to honor by illuminating the words of others: words that enshrine and encourage some someway brave, though somewhat frightened and fractured parts of the lives that we somehow lead, and lead together.

The lives we lead together, sometimes in the middle of the night, or of the day, when we least feel like we're together: when we feel most separated from the lives of others, most separated from the social world that we love and wish to be loved by in return. Many of us, I suppose, have encountered children who are not our own, but thought for a moment might be—like the little boy, outside the gym fifteen years ago, who smiled and waved a little at me, as if I were late, and he had been waiting a long time for my arrival: *immediately awaking, I found myself quietly seated in my bachelor armchair, where I had fallen asleep … [the boy] was gone forever* (Charles Lamb, "Dream Children: A Reverie"). All of us, I suppose, have encountered some form of the feeling of loneliness confessed in Lamb's bachelor essay, and sought one way or another to address that feeling, by finding some way of addressing others whom we can't, for one or another reason, face—sometimes writing across distances so long that we can't possibly expect to know for certain whom we are reaching, or even that we are reaching anyone at all. This effort to address a state of loneliness has for a long time now motivated the essay form (think of Francis Bacon writing with advice for courtiers from his position, after his banishment from the Court of James, of humiliated exile), just as it has motivated, for a long time now, forever practically, many other forms of writing as well. All this is to say that I know as well as I know anything that the loneliness at the heart of my project is not mine alone. The hunger for a feeling of connection that informs most everything I've written flows from a common break in a common heart, one I share with everyone I've ever really known.

Why this overmastering desire to communicate with others? (Virginia Woolf, "Montaigne"). And why does the desire to communicate with others most master us when we are least likely to feel sure that we can master *it*—the feeling of dumb fear that comes over us in the middle of the night, when it's too late or too early to call anyone? Everyone has his or her own version of this story, I am sure. Mine started suddenly, one summer, when I was young and had just begun to figure out that I wanted to write at the deep end of the pool. I had gone back home to my mother's house, to finish composing a manuscript that I really wanted to make fit for others to read. While there, I fell into the habit of waking up in the middle of the night, full of mild terror and sudden clarity about something that I had gotten wrong or left behind in what I had written the day before, something that had stalled my effort to communicate. Mission Statements and Major Mistakes that I couldn't see while the sun shone suddenly made themselves clearer than day in the full light of night.

The things that have called me from sleep have grown stronger and stranger over the years. Now they are feelings of error and of something missing as large as a lifetime and too vague to define, rather than missteps and omissions confined to yesterday's page or paragraph that wakes me up in the middle of the night (or sometime close enough). These are the feelings that assemble before the heart and mind of the middle-aged state, grieving and awaiting redress.

For a long time now, I've gotten used to going to bed early, and then waking up in the middle of the night, mistaking a crack of light at the bottom of my dream for the first light of the morning sun, feeling a little lonely and a little afraid, though not quite as I did when I was young. Now, I am mourning a little the loss of a life with others that I lived when I was younger, but which age and propriety will allow me to live no longer. Now I am moving toward losses (of my mother and much else) that I hardly know how I will bear.

It's a great relief to speak of those feelings now—even more than it was to speak to their youthful correspondents, way back when: the awakening pain has broadened beyond all page counts, but so has the feeling of peace that comes from writing my way through it.

That's because I feel pretty sure now that even while I'm writing in the dark, unable to see or even foresee anyone whom my words might reach, I'm not writing alone.

Partly, this readier feeling of togetherness gains its force through what is surely the most prominent technical, technological innovation to hit writing in a very long time: the essays that you see before you in this book, like the incessant communiqués to which I have subjected students in my classes and my college at all hours, especially early and late ones, over the years (*Professor, some of those messages you send out sound like Stream of Consciousness*, one young man remarked), those incessant communications that are the predecessors of these essays, were written originally on the Internet, where the prospect of access to the hearts and minds of others is as instantaneous as it is elusive. (In a moment, I'll have more to say about my sense of the effects of the Internet on the way we write now.)

I suppose that anyone familiar with the pleasures of texting, whether by means of the Internet or some other telecommunicating medium, knows the joy of imagining that what we write will reach those whom we hope to reach with the speed of an arrow or an electronic pulse. Few can resist the temptation of this joy. *Oh, people don't communicate anymore! They just look at little screens!*, my mother declared—my mother, brought up in a world where long-distance calls were measured by an egg timer and occasioned by little short of a birth or a death. And now look at her: she's First in her iPad Class! (*I'm very glad to know how to use this thing: now I know I can always reach your sister*, she has told me more times than I or any word counter could count.)

And, I suppose, anyone can feel the pang that attends the task of translating writing that originates in the liquid form of the virtual message, a liquid body of transport, quick-silvery as Mercury's wings, into the solid form of the book. This pang, though, is surely balanced by the intriguing desire to preserve at least some of the cargo communicated by those liquid means from dissolution into that very liquid.

A friend asks: *How can this form overcome the ephemerality of screen communications, which, once read, may never be read again, may even simply disappear?*

By "this form," my friend means the virtual one through which I have sought, over the course of many years now, to communicate as best I can. Communicate what, exactly? Most of all, I have sought to communicate some version of "me" to some version of "you," as near and as far as the closest heart. What versions of "you" and "me" exactly? Well, I don't know that I can say exactly: someone a little better, a little bigger, a little more than any mere self on a bad day (a lean and mean day): someone, rather, fit to join our best selves on our best days: the ones through whom all our unforgettable woe is a little forgiven and made a little finer, a little more fair—at least for as long as the flash of an image or the length of a sentence.

Can some record of these better selves (more and less than any specific self) be prevented from perishing the instant the image flickers away and the period appears, the period whose point it is to put the sentence to bed? Can those better selves be stored, so that they might last longer than a candle put out or a screen put to sleep?

Well, of course. But can such preservation surpass the mere solidification of the letters that form them? Can the spirit of those letters survive their migration from their first home, as near as written words can be, to the living and dying (always flowing) stream of spoken ones? Can those characters be more than so many frozen assets, filed memoranda—paper trails, trailing but never really reaching, the moving play of spoken love, made warm by the hope that you and I are always within earshot of each other?

And what about the pictures? What about them? As I mentioned earlier, all of the essays set down here, installed now in the bound book you have before you, were once paired with a picture. Most have not survived the migration. (Those that have are nestled mostly in the latter part of the book.) And they all seemed so attached to one another! All the little essays that I wrote were like so many (*so* many!) postcards—and what are postcards without pictures?—*flocks ... herds ... human face divine* (Milton, *Paradise Lost*). As I suggested earlier, it seemed to me implausible to include the bulk of those pictures: as implausible as it would be to bind all our words (no matter where we set them down) to a picture that would illuminate them: as implausible as it would be to imagine that our mother will have the wherewithal to watch over us for the rest of our natural lives.

While I believe that many of the messages that I have written to you are *sufficient to stand* (Milton, *Paradise Lost*) on their own now, without the pictures that have coaxed and conveyed them, I'll miss them just the same.

These are not easy questions, my friend remarks. But I cannot avoid asking them anymore than I can hope to answer them.

I can't help but be hopeful.

As to the images: a hope, hardly unprecedented, consoles me: the hope of the writer that the sights that he has cherished can be somehow installed in his very words themselves—those sights that have done more than words can ever say to bring those words into being:

thou Celestial light
Shine inward. (Milton, *Paradise Lost*)

As to the translation of words from liquid to solid form: I'm hopeful, here too. Recall all those voices you hear (voices, suddenly, that are, when you least expect it, *here*): the driest note, the deadest letter, giving way to the living spirit whose love, lit from within, will speak to you before the day is done.

In keeping with the common practice of the human heart (at least the heart that has made itself known to me), I have saved the hardest good-bye for last. As I have said, every essay in this volume was once attached to some particular image, made brilliant by the electric light of a computer screen. But the writing you have before you now was first lit up by something else as well, something from which it is most painful to part from that writing. The book that you have in your hands consists of writing that has been removed from its native society, and I would be wrong in more than one way were I to fail to acknowledge that society. I have alluded to this society already—at least I have mentioned its technological infrastructure: the invisible, partly audible and always felt community of readers made available by the Internet.

Many years ago, when I was still finding my way toward a midlife purpose (this volume is a partial record of that finding and that purpose), I received a message from a young man whom I knew only a little then, a message that helped me make my way.

Try as I might, I can't seem to recover that message now. The cost of someone such as me doing business on the Internet is all kinds of slips between cup and lip: all sorts of failures to send or save. But I have found that these losses do not matter very much. Take the loss of the message from that young man. That loss is hardly material: I remember the message, at least the heart of it, by heart. The title of the message was "Long Time Listener, First-Time Caller." Let me tell you: that was some first call. What did this young man have to say? Well, it may not sound like much when I say it, but it meant a world to me. He wrote to convey his approbation for what he saw me seeking to convey and encourage: *Only sincere sentiments, like this one!* That's what he wrote, sounding a little like the wounded hero at the end of *Great Expectations* who at long last returns home after a life of false pride, mortification, and exile to find, in his old place, a boy looking much like he did when he was young and before he was spoiled: *there … sitting on my own little stool looking at the fire, was—I again!* Now, why did my young friend's words sound to my ears like those of that resigned but still hopeful hero? I think because both are mild but quite amazed intimations of someone being somehow redeemed: both imagine a world where people can be their best selves, or do their best to claim and reclaim those best selves, anyway.

This may seem willfully blind or entirely foolish, I know. No one who has cast his eyes across the screens of the Internet—or the many cogent complaints about the deprecatory and delusive work that it can do to those who fall under its spell—can honestly avoid the suspicion that any community of readers formed by its virtual reach is at most a pale or engorged imitation of any community that anyone could imagine mattering. While I take such doubts to heart, I do not keep them there. I have been persuaded by many years of communication with many different kinds of callers that the citizens of the virtual world in which I have a stake, and from which the messages you have in front of you have been taken, can be just as virtuous as those who inhabit the world off-screen. The illuminated public sphere, as I have come to know it, whatever else it may do to the contrary, has helped fashion some of the best citizens I have ever known. These are the citizens of heart and mind whom I have sought to reach and who have, one way or another (personally, earnestly, critically), reached me. Everything I have written, I have written for them. They are present in every word that I now present to you. My gratitude to them surpasses evaluation. It is as difficult to decode as the screens of love itself.

This feeling of gratitude extends to include not only those who have been part of this writing for many years but also those who have been part of it only in passing. I shouldn't say only, since some of the intimacies that have best activated the writing I am presenting here have existed only in passing. And it turns out that the elemental ephemerality that attended the first appearance of the brief essays anthologized in this volume extends beyond the particular medium in and for which they were originally composed.

Reviewing what I have written to you over the past few years, I keep coming back to the feeling that it reflects and relieves the vanishing of a certain youthful hope. A friend my age said to me recently that she always felt like she was still in her twenties until she looked in the mirror. Well, the words I send out every day are themselves a kind of composite of that mirror. Sometimes I've wondered why so many of my morning compositions have felt like small acts of mourning something mildly big. What is the particular loss that generally marks and motivates what I've written over the course of our correspondence? Partly it is the loss of a once-crowded social world that I've already mentioned. But what I have written also marks the loss of something more intimate than that: the youthful hope (at least it was the hope of my youth) to have and to hold (and so to be held by) some continuous connection with some other party that would make both of us whole. Of course there are particular people and poems and points in between to whom and to which I return with something like religious regularity (like those birds whose migratory comings and goings my mother taught me to love). But I can no longer imagine that seeking to linger very long at any one time with any one of them would do any one of us much good. Thus the brief form that has engaged me so in recent years: the brief form of engagement by means of which I have sought to engage with you: the brief form of engagement that acknowledges the brevity of any human engagement with people and poems and points in between. Thus the nearness to tears that marks the beginning of so much midlife writing: as you get older, beginnings get harder and harder to tell from good-byes.

So much to love! So little time!

Reader's Guide

Stop this day and night with me and you shall
possess the origin of all poems,
You shall possess the good of the earth and sun,
(there are millions of suns left).

(Whitman, *Song of Myself*)

Well, I don't know about that. Neither of us have all day, much less all night, to spend with one another—too many prior and subsequent commitments (assigned background reading or backstories, the next hard test or bright text). And I sure don't have the keys to every poem and every promise of a new day. (Who does?)

But if you happen to have a few minutes to read what I've written, I hope you'll find that I've done what I can to make it worth your time.

I'm sure you'd do the same for me.

In the spirit of the brevity that is the soul of the intellectual hospitality I have sought to enshrine in these notes, I hope that you read what follows in any way, at any length, in any order, at any time (day or night), as often or seldom, and by any light that you like. I hope you will think of them as you would a moderately eccentric but pretty reliable friend who always happens to be around if you find yourself, in the midst of the business of your day and night, and the bustle of your moods, interested in hanging out for a while. You know that friend: his head is filled with all kinds of designs—but none of them are designs on you. He doesn't expect you to stay for long, or even necessarily visit very often, though he's always happy to think you might be visiting, and happy to think that you will stay for as long as you like. His house is filled with curiosities that he loves showing. And he's rather curious himself, and half the time, what he's saying—well, half the time, what *is* he saying?—he's not trying to trap you or trick you into staying longer than you like. Of course he wants your affection and your company, just as he wants to give you his. Mostly, though, he's trying to figure out what it is that he can do to make you feel sturdy and light in the midst of all our woe and wonder. When you do that, you make him feel sturdy and light himself.

note book

AUGUST 2007

195. “one of the people upon whom nothing is lost” 1

H. James

But what if the cost of being one of those people is that you yourself get lost yourself? Maybe such a lethal price tag can be avoided by careful shopping. I’m not by nature a careful shopper myself, but you try to learn what you need to learn before the learning comes too late.

Note: “I want so little—no new clothes—and I will learn what everything costs” (Eliot, *Middlemarch*).

OCTOBER 2007

2 **256.** ***Nora inu*** **(Stray Dog)**

Kurosawa (1949)

Telling lingerings on sights and sounds where the human factor has just vanished: a mechanical toy set in motion by children who only a moment ago wandered from the range of the eye; a torn white dress, still bearing the signs of the body from which it was stripped, the body so suddenly, violently pulled off-screen; confessional writings whose author has made his tracks right before they are read by his pursuers; a gun or a song made invisible once they are heard. It's like the History that Kurosawa's camera frames in all but words: effects that surpass by far the designs of those involved in the events that caused them—the theft of a pistol or a War Without Mercy—acts or Acts whose dramatis personae vanished in a sudden flash and whose half-life, no matter how long after, makes us feel like they have hardly left.

NOVEMBER 2007

336. “the clear architecture / of the nerves” 3

F. O’Hara, from “Early Mondrian”

Whatever it is, we always depend on the kindness of the strange. I’ll try to explain, but not too hard, because I think that you know what I mean, and I think you know what I mean because I think everyone knows the feeling that is my meaning—the feeling you have, say, when you wake up in the middle of the night, all alert to the beat, beat, beat, drip, drip, drip of some more or less mild dread. Such dread carries a sense of clarity without content—like the mere shapes and lines of the most abstract expressions, and a feeling that any comfort which will visit this dread can only come by granting it content. With luck, practice, and fortitude we can spin this unhappy hour, this hour of lead, into an hour of gold. That clarity, so entangled with fear, joins Wonder as the Foundation of Philosophy. That fear, so entangled with clarity, is as much the call of the wild, from the wild, that draws our ship to sea, as it is the citadel that protects us from whatever Foreign Fleet sets anchor near our shores.

DECEMBER 2007

4 **382. We Have to Be Careful about the Words We Use**

because they can't be careful about the way they use us.

JANUARY 2008

442. The Strength of Weak Gods 5

The ones vulnerable to pique and placating; the Jealous ones, and not simply for some bloodless principle of Monotheism; the one whose wrath at his People relents at the thought of ten righteous men amongst them; the one whose woundedness is the very currency of his strength, even before its Resurrection as Sign of His Condescension—the ones who allow us to say, "Maybe I can do that; maybe I can endure. Maybe I can do better than endure."

Note: Those familiar with the great work of Mark Granovetter—"The Strength of Weak Ties"—will see what I am up to here. The strength of those ties: where weak bonds that are the fabric of modern society's *gesellschaft* are as much the means of a flickering intimacy as an attenuation of all intimacy.

467. "the unconscious critical acumen of the reader"

Trollope

—how much the unconscious energies of the writer must entrust themselves to it!—how much any such appalling demand for fine attention should drive a desire to be so attentive in return.

Note: "as you like" (Shakespeare).

MARCH 2008

595. "Partial Enchantments of the *Quixote*" (2)

Expert words on the compound charms of the world's most active and ingenious spirit of chivalry. Alfred Schutz on "The *Quixote*":

> Knight errantry is first of all a way of life. It fulfils a heavenly mission. Knights errant are "God's ministers on earth, and the arms by which His justice is executed here." In this iron age it is their profession to roam the world, righting wrongs and relieving injuries. But chivalry is not only a way of life, it is a science, more, the queen of all sciences.

Schutz means in the first place of course that the knight worth his sublime salt must know a lot about a lot—law, theology, medicine, organic chemistry, poetry, civil (and then some) engineering, philosophy. But chivalry is not only the incarnated aggregation of forms of knowledge modernity is accustomed to regard as quite separate spheres. More: it is the queen of all science. And here we must cowboy up—no matter the breed or species of our stallion—to meet the "meta": chivalry is the overarching science of the sciences, the principle by which disparate sciences are drawn into coexistence. No Hegelian ("we might be tempted to speak of a non-Hegelian dialectic"), Schutz, Quixote's sociological Sancho Panza, admires the overarching scientific accomplishment of the Grand Master of Chivalry (enough to withstand the slings and arrows of any Arch), not as a synthesis by which different ways of knowing the world are drawn together, but rather as a sturdy (though not invulnerable) Treaty which, tacitly acknowledging that these ways of knowing will always go their separate ways, devises a peaceful means of negotiation between them.

How to explain the difference between the landscape of chivalry from the ordinary world the knight encounters? Claro! Enchanters!:

> Thus, it is the function of the enchanters' activities to guarantee the coexistence and compatibility of several sub-universes of meaning referring to the same matters of fact and to assure the maintenance of the accents of reality bestowed upon any of such sub-universes.

Friendly or hostile, these enchanters rationalize without denying any apparent discrepancy: with the aid of these hermeneutic ambassadors, Don Quixote can walk amongst ordinary mortals, an avatar of "multiculturalism" or "cultural relativism," only franker than its contemporary iterations. (Quixote is not shy to assert his claim to possess the key to any final finding of what's really going on—his grasp of "determination in the last instance" of the Truth is as sure as it is singular.)

And the most malevolent of the enchanters who inhabit Quixote's Ptolemaic Universe is kindness itself, when we compare them to the condescending consumers who finally bring down the knight. As you will remember, or know soon enough, whether through the cruelty you encounter in Cervantes or somewhere else—somewhere I hope not too dark—what brings Quixote to grief is the crowd of amused readers he meets on his third expedition, the heartless and manipulative crowd who already know his story as a story, and would never consider giving his noble intentions the time of day that would make it possible to communicate with him, person to person, social being to social being:

> In order to humor him and to establish with him a universe of discourse, they build up within the reality of their daily-life-world a world of play, of joke, of make-believe and

> "let's pretend," which, so they hope, will be taken by Don Quixote as reality in terms of his private sub-universe. But since they never bestow upon their make-believe world the accent of reality, they cannot succeed in establishing a discourse with Don Quixote and, consequentially, they cannot enter a true social relationship with him.

But enough for now with all this distance and disrespect. I will leave barely mentioned Schutz's own chivalrous attitude toward Quixote's worldview, an attitude best sounded by his near silence about it at the end of his brief and devastating essay on the World-Historical disassociation of the social senses as it is dramatized in the downfall of the knight. Remarking the regent "reality" of the world, the reigning seeing of the world, Schutz falls into respectful reticence about the view of the loser—the defeated view of the knight become a baffled clown.

I will mention—by way of the most hopeful closing I know how to make here, as we leave the knight beset by such cruelty—a story, hardly mine alone, of the Love that arises with the sight of Quixote's heirs and defenders. The first month of my freshman year, I fell fast and hard for a guy in my entryway, and what I fell for was his outrage at the ill treatment Quixote received at the hands of those in the novel who found this best of men merely colorful and quaint: "They're just torturing him! They don't care about him! They just want to make fun of him!" Such noble engrossment in the noble engrossments of those once made strong, now weak, by the fictions of nobility! How could anyone help but love such devotion to an impulse as vulnerable as it venerable?

Quixotes all around us: stop this day and night to listen to them—they're here to rock our world.

Notes:

1. Alfred Schutz, "On Multiple Realities."
2. Alfred Schutz, "Don Quixote and the Problem of Reality."

APRIL 2008

10 711. Paradise Bereft: The Social Elegy of De Quincey

De Quincey on Milton:

> It is the key to all that lavish pomp of art and knowledge which is sometimes put forward by Milton in situations of intense solitude, and in the bosom of primitive nature—as for example, in the Eden of his great poem, and in the Wilderness of his *Paradise Regained*. The shadowy exhibition of a regal banquet in the desert draws out and stimulates the sense of utter solitude and remotion from men or cities. The images of architectural splendour, suddenly raised in the very centre of Paradise, as vanishing shows by the wand of a magician, bring into powerful relief the depth of silence and the unpopulous solitude which possess this sanctuary of man whilst yet happy and innocent.

The solitude De Quincey sketches out here doesn't sound very happy to me. Vanishing shows of architectural splendour make of paradise the sorrowful solitude of haunted ruins—a solitude bearing the scent of departed glamour rather than a primordial pastoral peace rendered vivid by the contrast with the noise of cities. For a long time now, Milton's readers have remarked where and how his sense of man's first seat is haunted by the feeling that there had been others who had occupied it before, aboriginal figures whose displaced presence is still warm—"Faunus haunting the bower, a ghost crying in the cold of Paradise" (Empson).

De Quincey adds a sociological pathos to this habit of recognizing in Eden "the porch of spirits lingering" (Wallace Stevens). First of all, they're not lingering: they have already vanished, all of them! all of them! "The shadowy exhibition of a regal banquet in the desert draws out and stimulates the sense of utter solitude and remotion from men or cities": I think what grieves and frightens De Quincey isn't the fall from Paradise arranged by the evil in and beyond men. I think it is the fall into solitude whether in a doomed Eden, a forlorn desert, or a suddenly silenced city. De Quincey on *Macbeth:* 11

> If the reader has ever been present in a vast metropolis, on the day when some great national idol was carried in funeral pomp to his grave, and chancing to walk near the course through which it passed, has felt powerfully in the silence and desertion of the streets, and in the stagnation of ordinary business, the deep interest which at that moment was possessing the heart of man—if all at once he should hear the death-like stillness broken up by the sound of wheels rattling away from the scene, and making known that the transitory vision was dissolved, he will be aware that at no moment was his sense of the complete suspension and pause in ordinary human concerns so full and affecting, as at that moment when the suspension ceases, and the goings-on of human life are suddenly resumed.

A solitude that clings like the memory of a vanishing, or the sudden resumption of "the goings-on of human life" that work to render its antecedent suspension vivid by the contrast; or the sense of loneliness that flourishes most in the crowd of the city, the sense of loneliness at the heart of the city that makes of it, for all its human density, the most perplexing wilderness.

Notes:

1. Durkheim on the city as the capital of modern loneliness.

2. Simmel and Benjamin on the pleasures of such loneliness.
3. “out on a quiet spree / fighting vainly the old ennui” (Cole Porter).

716. The Silent Correction Continues

at more or less the same pace as the silent erring.

MAY 2008

780. "so true" 13

> Truths ... are too often considered as so true, that they lose all the power of truth, and lie bed-ridden in the dormitory of the soul, side by side with the most despised and exploded errors.
>
> Coleridge, from *Aids to Reflection*

I take Coleridge's point here to be that the power of truth comes into being only in a struggle with an army or whisper of doubt. Its only hope for rescue from a listlessness worse than death, an absolute infirmity where it shares a bed with the least interesting mistake, is to make it new enough to take it out of the airless realm of the universally acknowledged.

Before I met him, my first boyfriend had another boyfriend. Sometimes, to recall the thrill of their romance, the two of them would go out to a club and pretend they didn't know each other, and act like they were meeting for the first time. *Genius!*

Note: "Power ceases in the instant of repose" (Emerson).

810. "Scars faded as flowers"

Stephen Crane

What a crazy little simile! It helps mark the overwrought and oddly amped transition from war to peace at the end of *The Red Badge of Courage* (1895). Strange pastoral, the peace that Crane describes; a peace that surpasses any common understanding, any understanding of the common. The weird guy at the center of the story has gained some degree of honor in the eyes of other men, and surpassed the need for more; he is happy and ready to leave behind (at least today) "the red sickness of battle," a redness, from where he stands, at least as much the color of shame as the color of blood. As he walks away from the field of conflict, he walks away as well from the fear that his cowardice will be found out there; as that field fades, so too does his term of service in the toils of social engrossment; by the end, all bets, all rules of engagement are off, replaced by a most wacky garden scene:

> For a time this pursuing recollection of the tattered man took all elation from the youth's veins. He saw his vivid error, and he was afraid that it would stand before him all his life. He took no share in the chatter of his comrades, nor did he look at them or know them, save when he felt sudden suspicion that they were seeing his thoughts and scrutinizing each detail of the scene with the tattered soldier.
>
> Yet gradually he mustered force to put the sin at a distance. And at last his eyes seemed to open to some new ways. He found that he could look back upon the brass and bombast of his earlier gospels and see them truly. He was gleeful when he discovered that he now despised them.
>
> With this conviction came a store of assurance. He felt a quiet manhood, nonassertive but of sturdy and strong blood. He knew that he would no more quail before his guides wherever they should point. He had been to touch the great death and found that, after all, it was but the great death. He was a man.

> So it came to pass that as he trudged from the place of blood and wrath, his soul changed. He came from hot plowshares to prospects of clover tranquilly, and it was as if hot plowshares were not. Scars faded as flowers.
>
> It rained. The procession of weary soldiers became a bedraggled train, despondent and muttering, marching with churning effort in a trough of liquid brown mud under a low, wretched sky. Yet the youth smiled, for he saw that the world was a world for him, though many discovered it to be made of oaths and walking sticks. He had rid himself of the red sickness of battle. The sultry nightmare was in the past. He had been an animal blistered and sweating in the heat and pain of war. He turned now with a lover's thirst to images of tranquil skies, fresh meadows, cool brooks—an existence of soft and eternal peace.
>
> Over the river a golden ray of sun came through the hosts of leaden rain clouds.

An old story: for a self bound up with society to escape society, it must escape from itself. The individuality of this flickering character, dubious from the get-go, is freed by the end of individuation altogether. The new world "of soft and eternal peace" is a world for him all right, except that this him has relinquished all characterizing borders: "Scars faded as flowers"—but whose scars? To lose the marks of pain is to lose the marks of the self.

A specific twist on an old story: getting away from a society whose defining badge is men at war can be as much murder as remaining there.

Notes:

1. "a lover's thirst"—what a crazy little phrase! Both what it purports to describe (a desire for images) and, before that, the very idea that a lover's yearning feels like *thirst*.
2. The pastoral escape from society this passage describes makes itself dense with abstraction.

OCTOBER 2008

16 1157. The Trouble with Aphorisms

—that they risk encouraging us to imagine that their wisdom is always quick enough to be ever-ready to electrify even after their canonization; that the éclat of a proverb is always inclined to burst out with fresh light at any morning's first light; that words set more or less in stone are still in a state of perfect preparedness, so that at the press of a button, they will move to move us. It's like the folly of thinking that even the longest history of a friendship, hardwired in the circuits that convey the sound of the voice of the friend, cannot fall to rust and ruin; the failure to know that every going-through-the-motions of a Ritual will secure the Transcendence it has been commissioned to accomplish; the failure to face the hard fact—and how ironic, since facing the hard fact is really the raw attitude of the Aphorism—that every time we say "goodbye" or "I love you," our aim may fail as we essay to shoot straight to the heart.

Notes:

1. I wonder if the formulaic coaxing of math teachers—show your work—recognizes the hazard I have sought to set out here: a labor theory of philosophical value.
2. A history of Aphorisms, I suspect, would require a more than aphoristic discussion of the relation between those genres of brief statements laurelled as complete, either as the most refined refinement of Common

Sense or as a deliberate rumor of something wise that surpasses all common sense (the parable, say).

3. Also, such a history would be obliged to consider the possibility that the apotheosis of the Aphorism anxiously compensates for and renders triumphant—comprehensive in its incompleteness—the specter of the Fragment that surely haunts it (see W. Benjamin, G. Steiner).
4. The aura of the aphorism: always the promise that it tells the hard truth; that it is the worded fate which teaches "a fatal courage." Sometimes yes, sometimes not so much. See note 5, and the sentiment that appears between the dashes in the last sentence in the main body of this note.
5. C. Brontë: "It is weak and silly to say you cannot bear what it is your fate to be required to bear." When this Johnsonian missile hits right, it gives you courage. At other times, for whatever reason, it leaves you cold.

NOVEMBER 2008

18 **1187. "What is truth? said jesting Pilate, and would not stay for an answer"**

Bacon, "Of Truth"

The shock of mild surprise that begins Bacon's essay carries with it a peculiar intimation: truth may require our care not only because it is important, but also because it may appear quite *un*important. It may be quiet and easily dismissed, like a shy guest or a slow talker, puzzled and out of place. The power of truth may reveal its luster only by the solicitous regard that earns the confidence of those who are accustomed to being snubbed; the power of truth may make itself heard only by a subtle compassion that knows how to draw out those who have been quieted by quicker tongues; the patience that discovers the truth may not be far from the patience that knows how to encourage people who are reluctant to answer a question the first time it is asked.

Sometimes you need to ask the question again, in another way.

Note: On epistemology as ethos, see L. Daston and P. Galison, *Objectivity*.

1203. Ciceronian Suburbs

It was the first time I saw my mother cry. She's not the crying type, and it's no wonder that the sight of her in tears would mark an epoch in my brief life. There is nothing I like better than talking about my mother, all about my mother, but she doesn't like it much when I do. This is because my mother is opposed to people sitting around talking about themselves, and in her book, this would include members of their immediate family, just as she is opposed to air-conditioning, concentrated wealth, other people doing your laundry, most cosmetics, long sentences, "high hat" easterners, graven images, extravagance, the lifestyles of the rich and the famous, vanity, and my megalomania (as opposed to her own, to which she is quite attached). My mother has always operated as a virtual branch of the government in my mind, an institution as stable as a state apparatus, complete with its own self-aggrandizing legends and language. Her every written message to me ends with "Love, Mother"—as in "Read this. I like this guy. He is objective [meaning the writer she so commends enjoys the indescribable epistemological felicity of being in accord with my mom's own views]. Love, Mother."

So my mom is not the sort of person easily shaken up, and the sight of seeing her so must have made its mark on me; the sight of her striding with curt ceremony to meet me in the front yard as I walked home from kindergarten; the sight of her, so young then, her eyes stern and full of tears, trying to give herself some sense of purpose, like the way wounded girls wind up addressing their pain by talking to their dolls. And she said to me, in her severest civic lesson tone, in front of the shrubbery she had planted: *Jeff, I want you to remember this day for the rest of your life. The president of the United States was killed today*. We joke about it now: it's one of our more settled, I suppose sacred, routines: *Of course I remember, Ma. And do you know why I remember?—because you told me to*. We joke about it now, but it was no joke on November 22, 1963;

not where I lived: on November 22, 1963, the house where I lived was a house of sorrow.

Now I'm pretty sure I know as much as most people about the crimes, cardinal and venal, of Kennedy and his cadre, not to mention his class—but I'm also pretty sure that none of that diminishes the something serious that by my count began to get lost when the mourning for him passed. And I'm sure that I appreciate the suspicion that surrounds the various campaigns to get us to make all kinds of investments in the Mighty and the Glamorous—*let us now praise famous men*—but I'll go to my grave believing that whatever grounds I've got for a social conscience were put down one morning in late fall, when a young woman—practically a child herself then, by my long calculations now—came outside to tell her son that the Prince had been murdered in Dallas. And I have to wonder what is gained by way of political education for the children of my class, that would be the middle class, now that the very idea of a Res Publica, a public sphere, is such a faint thought or bad joke; now that the loss of a leader barely makes it through a news cycle, never mind rating as a Day of Awe. I mean, really, do the nameless thousands "dying thus around us everyday" from poverty, hate, and greed get better exposure now that we've forgotten what it feels like to have our mothers appear amongst the rhododendrons, summoning us to a national grief?

I think not.

Note: November 22, 1963.

DECEMBER 2008

1229. "Cold!" 21

Gena Rowlands in *Gloria*, dir. J. Cassavetes (1980)

The story: Rowlands plays a practical and satisfied retired underworld consort who, for reasons quite beyond her, is thrown together with a central casting "kid," chockablock full of all the silent or barely spoken idioms that make him fit for life on the street. And a good thing, too: the kid, through unfortunate accident, is obliged to go it alone, his parent having been freshly gunned down by annoyed mobsters.

So predictable is the story's move toward Love that it's hard to disagree—at least at first—with Vincent Canby's uncertainty reviewing the movie:

> Whether or not it's supposed to be moving, I don't know. That's the sort of question that haunts each Cassavetes work. You can never be sure that what you're seeing is artful or artless.

In the midst of all this confusion, the comic relief featured in the film is more than usually relieving—it actually throws things into relief. Thus, early one morning—like around 8:13 or so, in the midst of a hard to figure out moral crisis—G. R. repairs to a bar somewhere in the Northern, Nether Regions of Manhattan's Far Upper West Side, in order to collect her thoughts. Such collection requires some potable refreshment. She orders a beer. The bartender, a little snide, a little not, asks her to specify the brand she prefers. Gena, uncharmed by this mildly amused and aggressive interference with her vital cogitation, lashes out: *Cold!* is her pitch-perfect, moll-superb, sarcastic response. In contrast to the scenes of dumb and ambiguous pain that roll through this movie like all the Refuse of a pre- and post-gentrified New York (the film is not only made in 1980, it is set there as well), such pushback truculence is like a cold bath of clarity: such irritation is the currency of social relations as familiar as the subway line you know in your sleep. If this exchange distracts Ms. Rowlands from her moral meditation on her responsibilities to the kid, it also concentrates it, rendering it, by the force of its contrast, more real to her and to us. If we are inclined, despite Mr. Canby's creditable doubt, to be moved by the tale of Redemption, surely this inclination to be so moved has something to do with the sight of Gloria getting pissed off in the midst of the scene cast as the moment of redemption.

I do not doubt that "the consideration of death has been always made use of, by the moralist and the divine, as a powerful incentive to virtue and to piety." But as the author of this remark knows full well, any useful clarity that issues forth from this obscure consideration has roots, as superficial as they are vital, in less solemn annoyances that, dwelling on the surface of our daily business, is thus exposed to all the light of day. It's like Gena Rowlands in that bar, the darkness of where she has come to rest exposed to a rising sun of an ordinary day that no amount of cigarette haze or window-encrusted dirt can fend off forever. We are accustomed to regard our diurnal actions and affects as matters that arise from and are best explained by dark and deep motives, good, bad or indifferent. But shouldn't we credit as well the powers of our well-lit surface life as the sometimes antagonistic source and illumination of what lies beneath? Don't we do our best thinking as much in the midst of "the roaring traffic's boom" as we do in "the silence of [our] lonely room"?

Notes:

1. "The consideration of death has been always made use of, by the moralist and the divine, as a powerful incentive to virtue and to piety" (*The Mirror* 72, January 15, 1780).
2. On the soul as something brought to bloom by pushback efforts to defend the grounds where its garden might grow, see G. Simmel, "The Metropolis and Mental Life."

24 **1295. “Age does not improve us”**

E. M. Forster

—except when it does.

FEBRUARY 2009

1340. The Afterlife of Moles 25

My mother just hated them—moles, I mean—and if you were a child of hers, your earliest premonition of Ahab had to be the sight of her, out in the backyard, smoking, frowning, and plotting to destroy her own version of the White Whale. It was trench warfare: the moles would dig up the yard, pissing my mother off, big time, and my mother would stick garden hoses into the underground passages through which they, the moles, would go about their business, and whose upward and visible signs were the mounds of dirt that would drive her, my mother, to a state of more than domestic Fury. And then, having set out the means of flushing out her enemy, she would sit back, shovel in hand, watching and waiting, waiting and watching.

She got one once. My brother, four or five at the time, overheard her describe her gruesome triumph to a neighbor.

"Mommy, do Moles go to Heaven?"

"I hope not!" she replied with confusing candor.

"Why did you say that to him?" I asked.

"I had to tell the truth!" she answered.

And she does. Always—have to tell what she regards as the truth, no matter what.

Note: What's there to add to the Truth?

1341. "In the society of their common danger his innocence might serve to protect him"

Montaigne, "Of Solitude"

In this essay, Montaigne seeks to gather near the company of ancient philosophers who regard the most extreme solitude as the sole means of utmost good, the only really solid tax shelter, where we are certain to be unencumbered by any

importuning that would distract us from the calm and clarity that, according to their estimate, is the currency of the single secure value available to us.

Getting there is quite a trip, one replete with all kinds of backtracking, real or apparent. Thus, on the road to the Absolute Hermitage, we are struck by human, maybe even humane landscape, that seems to signal a move in the wrong direction. Crowds are contagious, Montaigne reminds us, and so if you happen to, or have to be, in one, you'd better be super careful:

> Merchants who go to sea are in the right when they are cautious that those who embark with them in the same bottom be neither dissolute blasphemers nor vicious other ways, looking upon such society as unfortunate. And therefore it was that Bias pleasantly said to some, who being with him in a dangerous storm implored the assistance of the gods: "Peace, speak softly," said he, "that they may not know you are here in my company."—[Diogenes Laertius]—And of more pressing example, Albuquerque, viceroy in the Indies for Emmanuel, king of Portugal, in an extreme peril of shipwreck, took a young boy upon his shoulders, for this only end that, in the society of their common danger his innocence might serve to protect him, and to recommend him to the divine favour, that they might get safe to shore.

I wonder if you're with me: I, for one, find the sight of the viceroy taking a boy on his shoulders, in the midst of great peril, pretty amazing, and hardly comprehended by any calculus of self-interest, ancient or modern, with which I am very familiar.

I wonder if you're with me in suspecting that something other than the usual calculations of looking out for *número uno* are at work in an arrangement that could well keep the kid dry while the potentate sucks up water. I wonder if you're with me in thinking that even the most lockstep or devious path to the Capital of Self-Interest may get sidetracked by a love of others so devious that it defeats even the stratagems of self-interest; a love of others that may prove to be the royal road to the greater good after all.

1349. "But I shall see it reanimated"

Walton, *The Life of Dr. John Donne*

Walton speaks received doctrine here, which, of course, supplies its own comfort and joy, but reading this, I was lifted up by something else for a second. This something is no doubt rooted in the standard promise of Resurrection canonically tendered here: the routes from that promise to various renaissance, romantic, and modern renovations of a fatigued sense of sight are well marked. Less definitely delineated is what is lost in these translations. And what is lost, precisely, must be lost, because it cannot be defined. This loss is as much cause for celebration as consolation. What is "it" that "I shall see reanimated," according to the more or less secular renderings of Scripture? What is "it" whose promised revival is magnetic enough to draw forth any Magi of the heart and mind to that momentary jubilee of joyful anticipation, followed by the equally brief funeral service for the foretaste of that revival, a foretaste that fades the instant it is coaxed by our teasing mind to venture out of the sweet session of a swaddled infant thought and expose itself to the cold air of explicit hope? What is "it" whose reanimation we never really cease to hope to see?

Isn't it everything, grown vague now, that we hope to see vivid again?

Note: "He was earnest and unwearied in the search of knowledge, with which his vigorous soul is now satisfied, and employed in a continual praise of that God that first breathed it into his active body: that body, which once was a Temple of the Holy Ghost, and is now become a small quantity of Christian dust:—

But I shall see it re-animated" (Izaak Walton, February 15, 1639).

MARCH 2009

1388. "The Unteachable Monkey," "The Fables of Panchatantra," "Indian Humor"

The Wisdom of China and India, ed. Lin Yutang (1942)

Inspecting my mother's primary bookshelf, one last time, before my second sleep and flight home, I realize with a mild start that I perform this ritual whenever I am about to leave her. And that's right: these books, a small community library, are the bibliographic correlative and component of her moral competence. Of course I open these books almost never. Most are very old and unpleasant in appearance, and by the looks of them, to my impatient eye at least, not at all "my bag"—Pearl Buck novels; heroic accounts of Andrew Jackson, depicting "Old Hickory" as a paradigm populist; atavistic exposés of power elites, et cetera.

In a rare impulse, I take one of these books down from the place where it has rested unnoticed for decades—Professor Lin Yutang's tome, cited above. A smooth and surprising volume, filled with all manner of familiar and unfamiliar satire and solemnity.

Reading along, I come across the story whose title forms the title of this note. The story is amusing and enlightening enough—all about a monkey whose resistance to helpful instruction becomes sufficiently violent to murder the emissary of enlightenment. I am struck more, though, by the wilderness of *teachable* monkeys the title of this anecdote obliquely surveys.

I hope I am one of the teachable ones. My mother, I suppose, thinks that I am, but mothers often give their children the benefit of the doubt.

Note: In fairness to her, she is hardly uncritical on the subject of Andrew Jackson.

1389. "stippled Hopkins"

Nabokov, *Lolita*

The poverty of perversity—not the sort that seals a connection with one or several others, but the strain that shuts you out from them:

> for I often noticed that living as we did, she and I, in a world of total evil, we would become strangely embarrassed whenever I tried to discuss something she and an older friend, she and a parent, she and a real healthy sweetheart, I and Annabel, Lolita and a sublime, purified, analyzed, deified Harold Haze, might have discussed—an abstract idea, a painting, stippled Hopkins …

These "genuine things"—well, at least the lost soul who speaks of them here hasn't lost his faculty to revere what he has lost. How weird, how "counter, original … strange," that the smoke arising from his own private Inferno, smoke from flames that will surely engulf whatever lasts about his being, should merge with the warmth of the "genuine things" from which he feels, and properly so, "forever banned"! They merge over the splash of a fish—"stippled" Hopkins: *rose-moles all in stipple upon trout that swim*. What, aside from the difference between Joy and Regret, separates the ecstatic eye able to get wet enough to seem to see right next to them, "rose-moles all in stipple upon trout that swim" from the dry beyond tears eye able to see only from a vast distance what is Adorable about that first eye? I think we know. I think the lost one tells us. The lost soul who speaks through Nabokov supposes himself—and we're right there supposing with him—the subject who knows. And what does he know? He knows that the loving eye who came before him has joined the dappled thing he loved, a commingling, a communion that might be most concisely measured as the opposite of owning—*GLORY be to God for dappled things!* (Hopkins, "Pied Beauty").

Note: Thus, *Lolita* as a critique of a spirit of appropriation well documented by C. B. Macpherson, *The Political Theory of Possessive Individualism: Hobbes to Locke.*

APRIL 2009

32 **1402. “And I am out on a limb, and it is the arm of God”**

Frank O’Hara, “Olive Garden”

I wouldn’t have imagined being out on such a limb when I was younger. Whatever had to go missing to get here—well, I don’t miss it now.

Note: “I cannot miss my way” (Wordsworth, *The Prelude*).

1418. “They just look at me blankly”

The Author’s Mother

Raised Protestant, the mother of the author of these notes is also a firm believer in the separation of Church and State. For many of her generation, no matter their theological or ideological stripe, the Establishment Clause was as Sacred as the Ten Commandments.

I mention this by way of Prologue to a brief Exchange that took place between the author and his maker (aka his mother), not more than twenty minutes ago:

Jeff Nunokawa: “Wow, Ma! It’s Good Friday!”

The Author’s Mother: “I’m perfectly aware of what day it is. You know it’s a State Holiday here?”

Jeff Nunokawa: "Isn't that a violation of the Establishment Clause?"

The Author's Mother: "That's what I'm always telling people at work. I say to them, 'What the Hell!? This is Unconstitutional!' They don't care. They just look at me blankly. They just want the day off!"

Notes:

1. The Establishment Clause—the first clause of the First Amendment: "Congress shall make no law respecting an establishment of religion."
2. A Perspicacious Reader will remark that the Mother of the Author of These Notes cleaves to the Work Ethic historically associated with certain schismatics clustered on her side of the so-called Reformation. Thus, while contracting the reach of her Piety with one hand, she extends it with the other.
3. See M. Weber, *The Protestant Ethic and the Spirit of Capitalism.*
4. My brother and I like to remember how, when we were ill as children, our ma would say, "Get up and work off that fever!"

1422. "He began to repeat the same stories more than once a day"

The infirmities of age now began to steal upon Kant, and betrayed themselves in more shapes than one … he began to repeat the same stories more than once on the same day. Indeed the decay of his memory was too palpable to escape his own notice; and, in order to provide against it, and to secure himself from all apprehension of inflicting tedium upon his guests, he began to write a syllabus, or list of themes, for each day's conversation, on cards, or the covers of letters, or any chance scrap of paper. But these memoranda accumulated so fast upon him, and so easily lost, or not forthcoming at the proper moment, that I prevailed on him to substitute a blank-paper book.

De Quincey, "The Last Days of Kant"

So did the book remain blank—a placebo, in place of the social steroid (all that "prepping," as if for another Critique or Seminar, rather than anything like casual conversation)—that Kant, who had always prided himself (and by accounts of those close to him, for good reason) on his lustrous powers of talk, felt, near the end, he required to compensate for their weakening?

I hope that De Quincey, who acted as a kind of go-between that helped the easily mortified philosopher negotiate the real world, was as kind to him in his decline as his brief memoir of those last days suggests he was. I hope that others were as well. If they were, I have a pretty good idea of what was written in that book, written or read or written and read by that most consequential reader and writer, written in more or less invisible ink: *it doesn't matter.*

Notes: None.

1440. "The mind, intractable thing"

> even with its own ax to grind, sometimes
> helps others. Why can't it help me?
>
> Marianne Moore, "The Mind, Intractable Thing"

I think it must be a step in the right direction, a step toward the help she wants, to think of the mind as *the* mind and not *her* mind. It's like one of those working relationships where you don't expect your girlfriend to be exactly the same person as you, or to be exactly "yours," even if you wish it were so sometimes, and even when you can't imagine why she isn't.

Note: "years that bring the philosophic mind" (Wordsworth, "Intimations" ode).

MAY 2009

1461. "His jokes are no trifles" 35

> They are always, though uttered with audacity, and equally free with the Lord and the Peasant, they are always substantially and weightily expressive of knowledge and experience.
>
> Blake on Chaucer's Host, from *A Descriptive Catalogue of Pictures*

Telling is the felt need for the Apology: all good jokes share the power of seeming trivial to those who really enjoy them, and to those who really don't.

1476. "Ms. Arthur"

> Tina Fey

I do not suppose that I am alone in associating Bea Arthur, the distinguished comedian whose recent passing we remark with something more than simple sadness, and Samuel Johnson, the redoubtable and voluminous patriarch who defined, and defines still, an epoch in English letters. Bearing the crown of a besieged but almost imperturbable authority, their humors, while the source of abundant instruction and delight to others, appeared to supply little joy to the humorists themselves—both were too seeming stoic to find much consolation, at least overtly, in even the plainest pleasures of sadism.

How fortunate, then, that both have had, and have still, such fluent admirers. "The earnestness and tenderness" contained in Boswell's richly documented esteem for Johnson finds parallel in the mild excess of formality by which Tina Fey elects to address, in her eulogy for her, one of the matriarchs of her craft: "Ms. Arthur." Sweet. Right.

Dulce et Decorum.

Notes:

1. "I really came to appreciate Ms. Arthur and her timing in *The Golden Girls* in its syndicated-Lifetime-marathon incarnation. I thought, "Man, there's a lot of good jokes in this, and these ladies are really skilled" (*Entertainment Weekly*, May 8, 2009).
2. "earnestness and tenderness"—from a letter Johnson wrote to Boswell, dated June 3, 1782, and included by the biographer in his *Life of Johnson* (1791).

1488. The Finer Reaches of Monotony

It is not that the noble nature loves monotony, any more than it loves darkness or pain. But it can bear with it and receive a high pleasure in the endurance or patience, a pleasure necessary to the well-being of this world: while those who will not submit to the temporary sameness, but rush from one change to another, gradually dull the edge of change itself, and bring a shadow and weariness over the whole world from which there is no escape.

Ruskin, "The Nature of Gothic," *The Stones of Venice*

The same smell of the same flowers; your father's old stories; the timing of the traffic light outside your window; a friend's usual self-deceptions; his habitual seeing through yours; the one-trick pony, making the lonely round of a distant memory; the poem you've read a thousand times, at least. Practice loving them long enough, and then one day when you least expect it, the perfect apocalypse, as quiet as a blooming: *wait, this is different* or, maybe, better still—*wait, I'm different!*

Note: See G. Simmel on the debilitating addiction to the alacrity of change that dulls and defines modernity in *The Philosophy of Money.*

JULY 2009

38 **1566. "So they groped and shuffled along"**

Kenneth Grahame, "The Return of Ulysses,"
The Wind in the Willows

A small band of animal friends proceed in near-total darkness toward their goal. They grope and they shuffle: sometimes this is the only way to reach home and renew honor. It may not feel very heroic, but best to keep going.

1579. "That's wonderful, Sue. What are you studying?"

> "Everything. Art, mostly. I love it. I'm really happy." She glanced across the prairie. "Nancy and I planned to go to college together. We were going to be roommates. I think about it sometimes. Suddenly, when I'm very happy, I think of all the plans we made."
>
> Dewey looked at the gray stone inscribed with four names, and the date of their death: November 15, 1959. "Do you come here often?"
>
> "Once in a while. Gosh, the sun's strong." She covered her eyes with tinted glasses. "Remember Bobby Rupp? He married a beautiful girl."
>
> "So I heard."

"Colleen Whitehurst. She's really beautiful. And very nice, too."

"Good for Bobby." And to tease her, Dewey added, "But how about you? You must have a lot of beaus."

"Well. Nothing serious. But that reminds me. Do you have the time? Oh," she cried, when he told her it was past four, "I've got to run! But it was nice to have seen you, Mr. Dewey."

"And nice to have seen you, Sue. Good luck," he called after her as she disappeared down the path, a pretty girl in a hurry, her smooth hair swinging, shining—just such a young woman as Nancy might have been. Then, starting home, he walked towards the trees, and under them, leaving behind him the big sky, the whisper of wind voices in the wind-bent wheat.

Truman Capote, *In Cold Blood*

Is this "pretty girl in a hurry" running away from a place and a person who reminds her of past catastrophe that she can never really escape? There is no reason to think so. Quite to the contrary: there is every reason to think that her alacrity is all in the direction of a future unharmed by that catastrophe. She revisits it as often as we (I assume we're together, here) would wish her to: we certainly wouldn't want her to dwell very long within its sights; nor, though, would we regard it as wise for her to try to avoid them altogether.

And what about the man who lingers a little longer with the remains of the catastrophe that had drawn his life near hers; the man who lingers long enough to witness the receding figure of the girl; the girl whom he has no great expectation of seeing again—no more than she imagines seeing the girl whose unfinished life she bears in her own person? Well, I guess he has the easier part in this story. I guess it's easier to watch someone walk away from a past that should be passed, than it is to be the one who starts the walking away.

Note: “Horseman, pass by!” (Yeats, “Under Ben Bulben”).

1585. “I have loved you all my life!”

Dickens, *David Copperfield*

At moments of crisis or calmness, we don’t mind that this common sentiment makes no literal sense. (For starters, the woman, beloved by “you,” hasn’t even known, much less loved, “you” all her life.) The untenable, untethered testimony of the most familiar and mysterious claim of Love touches the heart when it is hurt or happy enough.

Hurt or happy enough, we take what love we can get. Maybe we give it too.

Note: “You?” (Chaplin, dir. *City Lights*, final frame).

AUGUST 2009

1608. "What hurts now, but might become love" 41

M. Hollander, "Friend Fever"

—like the ache of awe; like contradiction fatigue; like many becomings whose final shape you can never name.

Note: "How strange must I feel myself in foreign parts" (James Boswell).

1621. "Forth, pilgrim, forth!"

Chaucer, "Truth"

A word of swift direction spells out a state of being, a being alert and full of purpose and promise. If you didn't know you were a pilgrim before, an earnest wayfarer going from here to someplace you hope will be better than here, well you certainly do at the sound of the speaking; you do as soon as you hear the lifting voice, urgent but calm, telling you, by a single, repeated syllable, that it's time to leave, or time to return.

Note: "it's time" (T. S. Eliot).

SEPTEMBER 2009

1646. "I know where the wild things are—but I'm not telling"

Jeff Nunokawa

Sometimes the best directions are the ones not given.

1659. "bouquet of attention"

Norman Mailer, *The Grammar of Sympathy*

Norman Mailer on Hubert Humphrey's acceptance speech for the nomination of the Democratic Party, Chicago, 1968:

> Tonight ... he was not hollow but full. He had a large audience, and his actor's gifts for believing a role. Tonight he was the bachelor uncle who would take over a family (left him by Great-Uncle Baines) and through kindness, simple courtesy, funds of true emotional compassion, and stimulating sternness upon occasion of the sort only a bachelor uncle could comprehend ... he would bring back that old-fashioned harmony to his ravaged [family].

Trust me: if you were of the political persuasion and cultural temperament of a man like Norman Mailer, it must have required almost unfathomable intellectual ingenuity to appreciate Hubert Humphrey in August 1968. I mean, not merely to "lesser evil" tolerate him (although in those desperate heated days and nights after the Assassinations and in the midst of a hopeless war with which Humphrey was utterly associated, even the spirit of minimal abiding was in short supply); but to actually suspend your Hostility toward the Middle-Brow, Middle-of-the-Road, Midwesterner, Vice President of a discredited Administration—well for a fancy leftist artist like Mailer, we're talking a minor miracle.

Accomplishing such a moment of grace, Mailer has one advantage. Even when his subject is one he despises, he is seldom merely snide: when he ventriloquizes a way of seeing and being foreign or even disgusting to his own, he is never satisfied merely to sneer; no: he really wants to see this other being and feeling; and he really wants, by the best lights of free-indirect discourse, to tell the inside story of this seeing and being. This impulse takes flower sometimes, it seems, in spite of the grounds of the character where it is rooted: sometimes Mailer will gain the higher mount, the grace of sympathy, by talking himself into it: what begins in the dark soil of thickest satire blooms, as the words flow, into something fuller, something sweeter, something kinder. If you start giving voice to some quite other consciousness with something other than a single-minded impulse to be snotty about it—well, God only knows where you'll end up. Like here: in the midst of the bachelor uncle cartoon, "funds of true emotional compassion" suddenly report themselves for duty—the "true" compassion of Hubert Humphrey, and then, behind that, the "true" compassion of the man behind the camera; the "true" compassion of the man who records it.

The compassion of a writer who bestirs himself to find in a morally exhausted and universally ridiculed ruin of a man the aspirations that first set him forth, to find them and speak them out loud; the compassion that discerns and describes in the lineaments of a Lucifer-Ruin lines leading back to a once stout-hearted warrior for whom Civil Rights was "simple courtesy"; the compassion that reads through the bundle of embarrassing gestures at the podium the now disembodied consciousness of the man Muriel married; the man Muriel loved.

I sometimes wonder what happens when you and I practice to understand perfectly, I mean perfectly, the whole of the wounded consciousness of the ethically defeated and unlovely. I sometimes wonder what we might heal by such essays at being considerate.

Notes:

1. "My friends, to those who say that we are rushing this issue of civil rights, I say to them we are 172 years late. To those who say that this civil-rights program is an infringement on states' rights, I say this: The time has arrived in America for the Democratic Party to get out of the shadow of states' rights and to walk forthrightly into the bright sunshine of human rights. People—human beings—this is the issue of the 20th century. People of all kinds—all sorts of people—and these people are looking to America for leadership, and they're looking to America for precept and example" (Hubert Humphrey, speech to the Democratic Convention, Philadelphia, 1948—a very different night than that night in 1968. The twenty years in Washington had become this night property to harvest [Mailer, "The Siege of Chicago"]).
2. "sometimes, it seems, in spite of the grounds of the character where it is rooted: sometimes it seems as if Mailer gains the grace of sympathy by talking himself into it: what begins in the dark soil of thickest satire becomes, as the words flow into something else, something sweeter, kinder": think about the phrase "funds of true emotional compassion"—you can smell the corpse of the merely satiric, but then the word "true" intervenes, and the living body of true charity all at once announces its presence.
3. On the potentialities of the rhetoric of empathy, see G. Eliot and her critics.
4. See G. Eliot on the pen as a "thinking organ."

1663. "I am finally seeing, I was the one worth leaving"

Postal Service, "The District Sleeps Alone Tonight"

The Classic Romantic Contest always has a Loser—rules of the game. Two men compete for the same woman, or the other way around, or some other, other way around.

I wonder how often and how, exactly, those who lose at this game feel the outcome as the right one? And how often is that feeling of un-sore losing merely a coping with a fate that will not be evaded in any case? And thus, finally, how often is it the summit sense that the better man has won the ring, and the better man is not you?

OCTOBER 2009

46 **1708. "Merleau-Ponty's readers can know him; he has made an appointment with them in his work"**

Sartre

Especially when your days are busy with more pressing, more pushing and shoving, everyday appointments, it's a good idea to remember to prepare for far-off meetings with people you don't even know if you'll ever know.

No time like the future!

Note: "I stop somewhere waiting for you" (Whitman).

1724. Why Do We Fall in Words? In Order to Avoid Falling Ill.

Sometimes I get annoyed with myself when I consider how much time I spend engrossed in intense but ephemeral emotions—passing feelings of injury or anxiety, and then regret about the wasted spirit spent pondering those feelings. These notes furnish a happy and wholesome means of abbreviating the habit of making these grotesquely bad investments. The worst that can be said of them is that they are a harmless diversion from baser and more annoying obsessions. It is a practice of the self I am delighted to recommend to anyone.

Note: "In the last resort we must begin to love in order not to fall ill" (Freud).

DECEMBER 2009

1794. The Good Enough Elegy

The name of a son who died young, a name that comes and goes through the consciousness of his more or less surviving father, without warning, and without much apparent effect (as if all the force of loss were dissipated into the background noise of that word from our sponsor to which we pay as little heed as possible).

Until it's the only word in the room.

Note: "Rudy" (Joyce, *Ulysses*).

1818. "may be translated thus"

> Barbara K. Lewalski & Andrew J. Sabel, eds.,
> *Major Poets of the Earlier Seventeenth Century*

The phrase that forms the title of this note I extract from the record of the labor undertaken to translate an epigraph from Hesiod. A reader who cares for the apprehension of amplitudes may find this formulation more than narrowly indicative. The coming together here of punctilious, almost tremulous caution (although we cannot know for certain, Hesiod's lines *may* be translated thus), with an operational self-confidence (Hesiod's lines may indeed be translated thus—for surely, here is a rendering close enough to the original): the wary and sturdy forward motion of the careful textual scholar: it may be translated (a "person-to-person" call) thus: the problem of another mind as distant from me as the most distant planet, and as dear to me as the most outlandish promise of happiness—I can't figure it out anything like fully; I can't transmit it, or to it, beyond the shadow of the valley of doubt. I can only sound out a reading of it that will express at once my hope that I may draw near it, and my knowing that I will never know for sure that I have.

Note: "The epigraph, a quotation from Hesiod's *Theogony*, II, 21–28, may be translated thus: 'We know how to tell many false things true-seeming, but we know how to speak the real truth when we will'" (Lewalski & Sabel).

1824. "A written French that was at once rapid and cursive, quick to evoke images, and just as quick to revoke them"

Alain Badiou on Michel Foucault

What is amazing about a style of writing marked by the speed with which it proposes and rescinds an image? Maybe it's a sense of self-possession that transcends any anxiety to possess: a writing so fluent with figures of vision that it can afford to enjoy them without a pressing need to attach itself to any one of them. Like a friend who knows that she will see you again, when she needs to see you.

No need to be held "captive to a picture" (Wittgenstein), out of fear that if you don't hold on to it, you'll lose all pictures; no need to fear that the loss of this or that vision leads to the loss of all the visible world. No need for that.

JULY 2010

50 **2084. Home Reparations**

> Miss Bates, deceived by the mock ceremony of her manner, did not immediately catch her meaning; but, when it burst on her, it could not anger, although a slight blush showed that it could pain her.
>
> Jane Austen, *Emma*

A careless, mildly malicious remark, made just because you can; the sudden, fatally belated recognition that you have hurt someone helpless, someone you preferred to think beyond anyone's power to hurt or help. You know it's too late to undo the damage you've done, and it gets worse: you know that what you've done you might do again if you aren't careful to avoid it.

But she's so boring! And how could anyone so boring not know so?! She must know! Didn't you read somewhere that being boring is a form of aggression? That's it! Her dullness is a depth missile—a covert operation undertaken by a once proud Armada, a feeble, feasible act of hostility (feeble except for its seeming infinite persistence) performed by a Late-Hapsburg-Helpless Imperial Being, who, if she still had the ammo and army, would incarcerate you forever, rather than for the few minutes (it seems like hours), or the few hours (it seems like days), that she still has the fading savoir faire to detain you with one of her going nowhere, and so very not fast, so-called stories. That's it! All you did was return a little bit of fire! That's it!

But that's not it.

Note: “The everyday phenomenon of compassion … the quite immediate participation … in the suffering of another, and hence the prevention or removal of this suffering, is that in which ultimately all well-being and happiness consist” (Schopenhauer, “On the Basis of Morals”).

JULY 2010

52 **3027. "What the hell can you learn from Las Vegas?"**

The Author's Mother: A Play in Eleven Lines

The Author's Mother: What do you want for your birthday?

Jeff: I'm glad you asked. Two books by Bob Venturi, preferably early editions …

The Author's Mother: You'll get whatever edition is cheapest. …

Jeff: *Complexity and Contradiction in Architecture.*

The Author's Mother: Hold on, I have to write this down … "Complexity and *what*?"

Jeff: Contradiction!

The Author's Mother: *Complexity and Continuation in Architecture* would have been a better title.

Jeff: Yes, but that would have been a different book, now wouldn't it?

The Author's Mother: Yeah. A *better* book!

Jeff: Also, *Learning from Las Vegas.*

The Author's Mother: What the hell can you learn from Las Vegas?!

Note: You see my problem.

DECEMBER 2010

3095. "Why this overmastering need to communicate with others?" 53

Virginia Woolf, "Montaigne"

I used to think it was because I was good at it. Now I think it's because it may be my only shot at being good.

JULY 2011

54 **3359. "a service of love"**

Having lost a dearly loved sister, a grief-stricken brother also loses any scruple that would impede his exertions to cherish her memory:

> Once in Westmoreland I saw a case resembling it. I saw a ewe suddenly put off and abjure her own nature, in a service of love—yes, slough it as completely as ever serpent sloughed his skin. Her lamb had fallen into a deep trench, from which all escape was hopeless without the aid of man. And to a man she advanced, bleating clamorously, until he followed her and rescued her beloved. (De Quincey, "Affliction of Childhood," *Autobiographical Sketches*)

In the first mourning period after the worst nights, servants of love appear before your wondering eyes in parades of dark distress, licensed to come and go in costume as foreign and lavish as a species custom had heretofore deemed dumb, suddenly invested with the powers of speech. You wake in the morning to glimpse the receding shapes of their Mysterious Menagerie, a disbanding Solemnity, whose pomp and circumstance shatter into fragments and figments as soon as you see them, like so much broken Glass that no man, this side of the keeper of the key to all mythology, has the power to put together again.

It's a good thing you don't have to take on this impossible dream. But if the mother of the lamb approaches to importune you to help rescue her child from certain death, do not allow the strangeness of the situation to delay the action of your mercy.

Note: "Philosophy is really there to redeem what lies in an animal's gaze" (Adorno).

AUGUST 2011

56 **3397. “The loss of all hope ... does not deprive human reality of its possibilities; *it is simply a way of being towards these same possibilities*”**

Sartre on *The Sound and the Fury*

At least once a day I lose all hope. I lie down and sleep with the TV on, thinking about all the things I’m not watching, and wonder whether, if I wake up just in time, the channel I’m on will have a special report showing me just how, just now,

---

Note: “There’s another way out of this room” (*Mad Men*).

3399. “show of grief”

> Wakes are of special interest here, because persons longest on the spot will have “worked through” some of their affective concerns about the deceased, while at the same time they are likely to have been the closest to him and to be therefore held most responsible for giving a worthy show of grief.
>
> Erving Goffman, “Accessible Engagements: The Regulation of Mutual-Involvement,” *Behavior in Public Places*

Those in-between mournings when your heart's just not in it—those imperfectly present, tense mornings, when you've been awake for too long to feel much of anything—when your heart is missing in action from all its usual places, especially your favorite of its usual places—the place in the story where you are brought up to tell the story of the one you knew best to admire. How much easier it is to tell the ones about those you never or barely knew, and admired all the same, than it is to take your turn at telling the Story of Stories: the one about the one you knew well enough to love. You've got nothing to add to this one—except every value you've ever had added to you, and every one you've ever hoped to add yourself.

Note: "We'll / Stay in touch. So they have it all the time. But all was strange" (Ashbery, "A Wave").

3422. "It was not till they had examined the rings that they recognized who it was"

> When they entered, they found hanging upon the wall a splendid portrait of their master as they had last seen him, in all the wonder of his exquisite youth and beauty. Lying on the floor was a dead man, in evening dress, with a knife in his heart. He was withered, wrinkled, and loathsome of visage. It was not till they had examined the rings that they recognized who it was.
>
> Oscar Wilde, *The Picture of Dorian Gray*

It happens all the time: you work so hard pretending to be something you can't possibly be (*exquisite youth and beauty*, well past your fiftieth birthday, for example), that by the time the person you really are finally surfaces in full view, that full you is a total goner. And if you'd just let the half you've hidden see the light of day—who knows, maybe the two of you (the half doing the hiding and the half being hidden), put together, could have been fully a friend to you.

Who knows? Maybe it's not too late.

Note: "her hair down … like an early Methodist" (George Eliot, *Middlemarch*).

SEPTEMBER 2011

3427. "The Bondsman always labors in submission to the true master and Master, the fear of death"

Robert B. Pippin, *Hegel on Self-Consciousness: Desire and Death in the* Phenomenology of Spirit

You wake up in the dead of night, and your Lazy Susan of a Mind stops its slow spin, leaving in front of your consciousness a particular crevice of concern. (I'm having some difficulty assembling the right language to convey my meaning here—bear with me: you remember or have heard tell of those revolving platters [they were made of monkey-pod (least that's how I remember them—but maybe that was a Hawaii thing)], with dishes containing different kinds of food—maybe poi, or some kind of weird-ass polynesian salad or lomi salmon [no spam]—my memory is a little hazy here. I'm thinking these intriguing contraptions were around sometime in the early seventies, maybe, during the heyday of fondue and culottes.) Anyways, I digress: I'm malingering on the details, and all the while, I have a Job to report out—so enough already with the Lazy Susan. Getting back to the quarry of this meditation: you wake up in the dead of the night, and you're all *Jesus Holy Christ, I have so much to do! There's so much work I should have done, already! I'll never get it done. They're gonna* kill *me!*

So who, exactly, is going to kill you? According to the "existential fable" (Pippin) Hegel sets up, it's some primal master, who in a struggle to the death with some primal slave, wins the game of chicken (the p.m. is willing to die in the fight; the p.s. not so much, ergo the p.s. loses and, to earn his living, has to carry all the p.m.'s water, until such time that the p.m. is so dependent on the p.s. that the lazy Susan turns around).

But that's not the part of the story that I care about right now. Another part of the story is getting to me right now. I'm wondering if and when work can ever be liberated from the fear of death. I hope so. I hope soon.

LABOR DAY, 2011

Note: "Labour … blossoming or dancing" (Yeats).

3505. "Telephone Directory," "Heaven"

W. H. Auden

One could conceive of Heaven having
a Telephone Directory ("Postscript …").

We mostly don't call each other anymore. Not like we used to, anyway. And when we do, we mostly don't pick up. That's cool, though. It just makes us appreciate more the times we *do* get through. Now, when we answer, it's like the reverse charge of the *bye*, which always sounds like the beginning of the big one; it's like a hello from here, all the way to Heaven. That's why our hope goes way beyond the bounds of all area codes when we hear the ring at the other end of the line—

Note: "Stardust in negative, between the rings" (Merrill, "Mirabell").

3507. "She'd take it all for fun if I didn't hurt her, and that I can't do"

George Eliot, *Silas Marner*

How easy to recall a father, cruel; much harder to remember those times when he failed to be so—last-minute confusions of charity that softened a spanking or a grounding into a sentence as slight as the punch line of a forgotten joke; as sweet as the sign of a remembered peace.

Note: "this fair defect of nature" (Milton, *Paradise Lost*).

OCTOBER 2011

62 **3527. "gigantic broken revelations"**

George Eliot

Broken revelations: for the sake of the pain that you find yourself feeling for some hurt, her; a pain more like a continuing illness of the eye than any unenduring dark; more like a simply Given than a single Grief, let's think of the broken revelation as the dim realization that something you dearly love and wanted to see kept whole has been broken (a heart, a hope; a family or feeling of glass; an endearing, un-enduring sense that the World could never take leave of its senses). You're old enough now to know she'll probably be okay, but God, you're sorry that she has to swim through the strange sea that lies ahead—*the long vistas of white forms whose marble eyes seemed to hold the monotonous light of an alien world: all this vast wreck of ambitious ideals, sensuous and spiritual, mixed confusedly with the signs of breathing forgetfulness and degradation* (G. Eliot). She'll be confused for a long time: actually, you're old enough to know that the confusion will go on, one way or another, forever. You wish you could shield her from the blood-dimmed see—the breaking news, the breaking waves—but you know that you can't. The hits just keep on coming, and you just have to hope that she will learn to see, in the patterns of their breakings, the promise of a pathway home.

Notes:

1. "Our moods are apt to bring with them images which succeed each other like the magic-lantern pictures of a doze; and in certain states of dull forlornness Dorothea all her life continued to see the vastness of St. Peter's, the huge bronze canopy, the excited intention in the attitudes and garments of the prophets and evangelists in the mosaics above, and the red drapery which was being hung for Christmas spreading itself everywhere like a disease of the retina" (George Eliot, *Middlemarch*).
2. "Sólo él sabía [...] que su aturdido corazón estaba condenado para siempre a la incertidumbre" (Gabriel García Márquez, *Cien años de soledad*).

After the See-Change, you'll come home: we'll leave the lights on for you.

3528. "The secret discipline of imagination"

> The secret discipline of imagination is a double burden, discordant and harmonious: first, its delight in the power and freedom of art; second, the controlled surrender whereby it acknowledges the limits of artifice.
>
> Harry Berger Jr., "A Secret Discipline: *The Faerie Queene*, Book VI"

I've never thought of it that way, and, although I'm always on the lookout for the beautiful concession, I do not believe that I ever will. And this despite the fact that I know as well as I know how sorry that sounds, the sad and well-staged cases that would nullify my faith: there's that play where the great magician drowns his books; a wish whose fulfillment punctuates and punctures a dream; the brokenhearted novelist whose grief bleeds out in a last-scene confession that all his scenes are in vain—his high-piled charactery, mere puppet shows. What can I say? People lose their nerve all the time. I certainly do. Not as much as I did once, but even now, at this late date, I catch myself second- and un-guessing myself—contriving to "un-send," or to recur to a less voguish and even antiquated parlance, *retract* (like a nervous witness before an unfriendly committee), some act of fancy, high enough to fly right over this or that instated fact on the ground.

But then I remember the other side of the story; the side that Mr. Berger's elegant formula appears to have forgotten: the secret discipline by which the emissaries of fantasy, in the very act of deferring to it, quietly infiltrate the realm of the real:

> They all gave place when the signing was done, and Little Dorrit and her husband walked out of the church alone. They paused for a moment on the steps of the portico, looking at the fresh perspective of the street in the autumn morning sun's bright rays, and then went down.

> Went down into a modest life of usefulness and happiness. Went down to give a mother's care, in the fulness of time. ... They went quietly down into the roaring streets inseparable and blessed; and as they passed along in sunshine and shade, the noisy and the eager, and the arrogant and the froward and the vain, fretted and chafed, and made their usual uproar. (Dickens, *Little Dorrit*)

Such comings down root a stable garden of gladness, deep rooted enough for the perennial species of *sadness*,

---

Note: "a grief ... I remember ... when I laugh" (O. Wilde, "The Decay of Lying").

3534. "On pardonne tant que l'on aime"

La Rochefoucauld

Sometimes forgiving can feel like a foreign language or even a whole foreign country. Partly, if you've reached my state, that's because you've so expatriated yourself from domestic entanglements that whatever Wrongs you feel you've done, or have had done to you, feel as far away as Easter 1916 or Islands in a Stream of Unconsciousness. You feel like you've so forgiven your ancient-accented, foreign-familial past that it doesn't even feel like forgiving—more like just plain old forgetting.

But then I remember the love that *(who knows how?)* still keeps together that little grass shack called home, and that there's still a place for me there, whether I think I like it or not, and that place keeps getting bigger even as it's getting smaller, and somehow according to the same algorithm that proves once and for all that Hamlet is Father to his father, all this means that people are forgiving and being forgiven all the time, and you and me are part of that tidal wave that lifts all craft, whatever the rip of the anger we feel and fear, and anyway it's true—truer than most things, anyway—the Stuttering Bloom that rises out of *Ulysses*'s last big stops-all-pulled, bringin'-it-halfway-home donnybrook, somewhere around the Battle of Midway somewhere in Dublin and halfway to Hana that go-round with the half-blind-drunk rageoholic—you remember what the Wandering Jew says, even if you think you don't and think you never heard it in the first place sure you do I know you do because you and I we're family and we heard it all together on some same Sinai.

We were at the Bar together when he said It when (last call) he said

---

Note: "Love … I mean the opposite of hatred" (Joyce, *Ulysses*).

3540. "(Why is it such agony to meet people—at least sensitive people?)"

> Such embarrassment that all you can do is to hold some phrase in your hands as you go up to them to bridge that gap—a buffer to take the shock, like the ones you use for boats coming up to the docks. After the first bump it's all right.
>
> Anne Morrow Lindbergh

Or you go up to them empty but openhanded, and with those hands, or some other means of showing without telling that you *know* that they are sensitive (you *do* know that: everyone you've ever met, or ever will, is sensitive).

Take you: the things that go bump in your day, they blur into ache in your night, the ache of any lost chance to help beckon and beacon the arrival of an unarmed armada slipping silently in amongst the usual flaggings of more defined

and defended craft. You're sorry to be slow at any first sighting, and hope that the one lately spotted will take comfort in knowing that any "state of relatedness" "can be reached only through some kind of suffering and sacrifice … through trial and error." (Kurt Wolff to Anne Morrow Lindbergh)
Sometimes when you're really late (maybe too late) to take the meeting, as crazy as it sounds, you sort of wish you were sort of like an old town, vested with the broadest powers to receive in style even the quiet citizen, the displaced, unstated person; sometimes when you're really late (maybe too late) to take the meeting, you sort of wish you were sort of like an old town, an old city, and it was

---

Note: "as if the city were a human being, a good and dear trusted friend who had come a long way to welcome him" (Katherine Anne Porter, *Ship of Fools*).

NOVEMBER 2011

68 **3551. "I say, we good Presbyterian Christians should be charitable in these things"**

> and not fancy ourselves so vastly superior to other mortals, pagans and what not, because of their half-crazy conceits. … Heaven have mercy on us all—Presbyterians and Pagans alike—for we are all somehow dreadfully cracked about the head, and sadly need mending.
>
> Melville, *Moby-Dick*

Right? I mean, one way or another, we're all so many shipwrecks, right? I remember not that long ago clinging to the feeling of being Right, like a piece of one of those wrecks. What made me let go? I don't know exactly. Maybe the realization that the sea I was afraid would swallow me up was more likely a sign of all the tears that have ever been shed. We learn to deal with tides like that, right?

Note: *Lacrimae rerum.*

3570. "There are only two things: Truth and lies"

Kafka

Another thing: facing the fact that one will sometimes turn into the other. Oh, and forgiving them both sometimes when, try as you might, you really can't tell them apart.

Note: "I believe in truth though I lie a lot. I feel the pain from the push and shove" (Human League, "Love Action").

DECEMBER 2011

70 3597. "He glimpsed something generic and joyous, a pageant that would leave him behind"

> "I bet," she said, and raced to the porch, and in the precipitate way, evasive and pleased, that she flung herself to the top step he glimpsed something generic and joyous, a pageant that would leave him behind.
>
> John Updike, "Man and Daughter in the Cold"

You think you understand them, and you do a little (sometimes, you think, a little better than they understand themselves), but mostly you don't—your kids, when they're older, I mean; the ones big enough to take the Lift without you; the ones who sometimes still need you to give them a little time of the day, and then, mostly, for you to get out of their way. Of course, you *do* understand, at least a little, that they still count on you to think of them a little, pretty much every day. Or is it just that knowing a little that you count on them to count on you so, they are tender enough to oblige? I wouldn't put it past them (the cooler they play, the kinder, they say).

The pageant will leave you behind, all right. All right: there's always room at the Inn for the Launch Party, traditionally held the night before the departure of the Passion for Parts and Prospects unknown. "There were a lot of people there whom you would have enjoyed quite as much as I did,

Note: including the young James Merrill, who is about the age which you and I were when we were in New York" (Wallace Stevens to Witter Bynner).

JANUARY 2012

72 **3622. "the law of his heart"**

> The individual ... *carries out* the law of his heart. ... The law of the heart, through its very realization, ceases to be a law of the *heart*. For in its realization it receives the form of an [affirmative] being, and is now a universal power for which the particular heart is a matter of indifference, so that the individual ... no longer finds it to be his own.
>
> Hegel, "Actualization of Self Consciousness," *Phenomenology of Spirit*

I wonder about the fear that fills my heart on the eve of the Epic of its triumphant evacuation. Say the story is true: Say that once I put out of my heart what is into my heart—say, at the pitch of night, when I am most afraid (the time now): Then the heart that so fears ceases to be mine, and the fearer so fearful ceases to be me. If so, why be afraid, so?

Is it that I might be scared that you might be scarred by whatever it is beyond all sight that fills my heart with so much fright?

It's not that. I am certain that by the time this telegram reaches you, the terror that dictates it will have dissipated through the very fact of its conveyance. By the time it reaches you, I do not doubt that whatever ghost, which got me going to write you, will be long and a little enough gone. Whatever it was that so "harrow[ed] me with fear and wonder" (quoting

Hamlet, you can hear already—thank God—the ghost giving up), will be hollowed (hopefully halfway hallowed) into the very type by which it makes its way to you. At worst, what reaches you will cause no harm—merely a faint reflection of someone else's failed terror. And at best—a lot to wish for, I know, but well within the bounds of recorded human power—an object lesson in how men and women learn to become, a little bit, their better selves by the practice of renouncing their own "small … shivering" (George Eliot) specificity (a practice, never perfect—which of us self-respecting self-reliers would want *that?*)—renouncing a little the deed we hold dear as the native ground of our own particular souls.

So what now is it that still murmurs in the heart? Nothing now, I guess—dread and dreader, *being gone, I am a man again.*

Still, there's tomorrow night. *Still.*

3269. "He somehow felt he was headed in the right direction"

> As he peered ahead into the great land that stretched before him, the way seemed long. But the sky was bright, and he somehow felt he was headed in the right direction.
>
> E. B. White, *Stuart Little*

His search for the bird he loves best having stumbled, a little pilgrim, susceptible to just about everything that the world has to throw at him, but pretty sturdy still, is helped up and set straight by a Good Samaritan, a roadside repairman who is there to remind him that "a person who is looking for something doesn't travel very fast."

His doubts were his own property (Isaiah Berlin on John Stuart Mill)—but the directions that help any kind steward, no matter how doubtful, toward his destination: well, that comes from gifts you only get once you've given them to someone else.

Note:

> The symbol star it lifts against your ceiling
> Help me accept its fate with Christmas feeling.
> (Frost, "The Gift Outright")

3270. "I track my uncontrollable footsteps"

> ... while they take their quick turn, even on stealthiest tiptoe, toward the point of view that, within the compass, will give me most instead of least to answer for ...
>
> Henry James, preface to the New York edition of *The Golden Bowl*

I can answer for this much, concerning my nocturnal movements and moments of seeing right now: never, in my weirdest dreams, did I imagine that Late-Night-Life would look as crazy as this. It's as crowded and busy and hard to figure as it was back in its bright-lights, big-city phase and, in its own way, no less hazardous. (No wonder I sometimes get so tired during the day. My late-night running mate from that earlier dark age used to say: *it's like having a second job!*)

The mysterious calculating of seeking strangers across a crowded, darkened Club has been replaced by the wily ambiguity and willful allusions of the hooded ancestors, as they conduct themselves across a space of time and text as dim and demanding as any distant-starlit desire to close the distance—that desire so defining the transports and compass of youth ... and age. On the bright side, you sure save a lot in cab fare and faring—one thing I still remember, clear as day: getting from the west side to the east side and back again could be murder on your pocket and your peace of mind. Nowadays, everyone you want to see, and everyone you don't, and everyone you do and don't—the gang's all here. No need to go out and seek them—like Chinese Food and Trouble, they're perfectly ready to come to *you*. No need to go out to seek them: the mission now is to really see them. They come to you now, crossing your threshold, and whatever courage inheres in simple courtesy requires that you greet them at the door.

There's a problem, though, when the party comes to you, now: you don't really know their language anymore: a dreamy demotic that has faded from the sphere of your familiars. So the lot to answer to—all those now masked faces you once (or wished to) love; all those precedent principles and principals to whom you pledged your allegiance (maybe you were just reciting at first, but not at last)—the Lot you Answer to, what with all the weirdness of its messaging and the consequent weirdness of your mirroring, is a Lot to Answer *for* (gaps in your transcript; flawed and failed translations; excesses or inefficiencies in formalities and familiarities).

Whatever. *In dreams begin responsibilities:* It isn't easy, but you try. So much of the company seem so strange now—but don't be scared. Just welcome them as brightly as you can. "Subsidence of the fearsome ...

Note: was always, at first, positive emergence of the sweet" (James, *The Golden Bowl*).

3272. "the masked pain of his bewilderment and solitude"

> Who that has had experience of our social reality will doubt its alienated condition? And who that has thought of his experience in the light of certain momentous speculations made over the last two centuries ... will not be disposed to find some seed of cogency in a view that proposes an antinomian reversal of all accepted values, of all received realities? But who that has spoken, or tried to speak, with a psychotic friend will consent to betray the masked pain of his bewilderment and solitude by making it the paradigm of liberation from the imprisoning falsehoods of an alienated social reality?
>
> Lionel Trilling, *Sincerity and Authenticity*

I'll bet a lot of people will remember the post-1960s intellectual sentimentalists Professor Trilling takes his stand against here (the pro-crazy crowd—R. D. Laing, Deleuze and Guattari, *inter alia*). On the other hand, aside from me, there are only three people in the world who know or knew the story I'm about to tell you, and two of them are dead, and one of them would never tell. Here's the story: There was a lady who lived across the way from us when I was a kid, and I loved spending time with her. So engrossing was the companionable compassion of her conversation that I really can't remember what the other kids were doing while I was spending all those hours talking to her. All I remember is what sure felt like the sincerity and authenticity of her engagement with me. I would follow her around while she performed (or didn't) her housewife chores (usually with a cigarette dangling from her mouth), telling her about what made me afraid (mostly my father), and listening to her tell me that I was stronger than I thought, and that I didn't need to be so afraid. (*Your father loves you*, she would say. *I know your father, and I know that he loves you.*)

And here the story goes south: her husband lost his job, the family lost the house, and she lost her mind. Her husband left her, the kids were taken from her, and she was moved to some kind of halfway house. My mom and another neighbor lady used to go visit her when they could, which wasn't as often as they thought they should, and still more often than they really wanted to: in the last years, she was mostly locked in her private madness—all traces of the hilarious charismatic my mom and the other neighbors remembered as the most magnetic social force this side of Pearl Mesta were pretty much worn away by then. Sometimes, though, she would break free of her personal prison for a few minutes, and remember the old days. It was on one of those leaves of lucidity that she told the story about how when I reluctantly left her house (she had to send me home—it was dinnertime), I would walk backward, so that I might keep her in my sight for as long as I could.

I just kept looking back. Still do, sometimes.

3281. "Add the case that you had loved her"

> ... and had made her the subject of those poor dreams which have, at one time or another, been in the heads of more men than you think likely.
>
> Dickens, *Great Expectations*

Those poor dreams of a passionate love saving a world or making a marriage; those poor dreams, whose least memory suffices to coax their most seasoned denier to relent long enough to soothe a boy caught still in the mourning mist of them; those poor dreams, whose every defeat (despite all odds and most appearances) can serve to strengthen the decency of the defeated; those poor dreams: perhaps not so poor, after all.

Note: "The evening mists were rising now, and in all the broad expanse of tranquil light they showed to me, I saw the shadow of no parting from her" (*Great Expectations*—the second ending).

3283. "grief for disappointments of no fatal consequence"

> Samuel Johnson, "Rambler, 68"

However differently we may feel while we dwell in their midst, most of our disappointments are of no fatal consequence. We miss a commuter train or a connecting flight: there are more where those came from, and one or another of these will eventually get us where it is we mean to go. The lecture we gave today failed to find the key of clarity we hoped it would: we can right its rail and reckon its resonance when the class next meets. A conversation with an old or new friend that begins with the alluring promise of escalating and unexacting candor ends in a feeling of awkwardness (have we said too much or too little?) that annuls the joy of that promise: next month or next meal, that feeling of awkwardness will give way to the ease of a new intimacy.

Of course, no one remotely dedicated to the practice of honesty will deny that some disappointments are quite indelible, but even these, however much they might depress the spirit, seldom involve the deprivation of a life. Few of the incurable disappointments we feel in ourselves or others bring death into this world, or all the woe pertaining there.

It will nevertheless be admitted, by any feeling mind, that we are likely to grieve, as if for a death, these irreversible cancellations of underwritten hope (typically a promise of happiness contained in a feeling of excitation, tenderness or esteem): *A thousand miseries make silent and invisible inroads on mankind, and the heart feels innumerable throbs, which never break into complaint* (Johnson, "Rambler, 68").

And while these silent disappointments might be made to seem larger than they are when those who feel them speak of them too much, they are surely made to seem less so when those who suffer or see them fail to speak of them at all. Even the least sense of being let down and left to fall behind by those we once may well have deemed better than ourselves, or our own better selves, will serve to remind us that we will be obliged soon enough to take our leave altogether from those whose voices, or laughter, or gestures we love—or from those whose voices or laughter or gestures we have loved *(even losing you)* (Elizabeth Bishop, "One Art") and already, or all but, taken our leave.

3287. The Human Part of Speech

> I knew one that, when he wrote a letter, he would put that which was most material in a postscript, as if it had been a bye-matter.
>
> Bacon, "Of Cunning"

By the way, he said, slowly circling back round again, after we had made our formal farewells (I wonder if either of us knew then how seldom we would meet after that summer—so long ago—we had spent becoming the best of friends),

---

Note: *meeting you was the high point of …*

3299. The Elements of Sympathy

> All through *The Elements of Style* one finds evidences of the author's deep sympathy for the reader. Will felt that the reader was in serious trouble most of the time, a man floundering … and that it was the duty of anyone attempting to write English to … get his man up on dry ground or at least throw him a rope.
>
> E. B. White, "Will Strunk"

By the points of my compass, the high and dry place from which I'm supposed to throw the rescuing line dwells smack dab on the grounds of grammatical fiction, *a language game which we cannot learn* (Wittgenstein). I mean, how would I know that you needed my help if I didn't know that I needed yours? My father used to warn us that we couldn't rescue someone from the water unless we ourselves were in no danger of going down. Nowadays, though, I pretty much feel that I'd have no hope of helping to save someone if I weren't at least a little scared of being lost myself.

Note: "And Gide is surely mistaken when he ... say[s] of ... characters that they are 'desperately mundane' because 'they never live except in relation to each other.' It is just in their relations that they live so bravely, and are so little mundane" (F. W. Dupee, *Henry James: His Life and Writings*).

3302. Tradition and the Individual Eavesdropper 81

> Kafka eavesdropped on tradition. ... The main reason why this eavesdropping demands such effort is that only the most indistinct sounds reach the listener.
>
> W. Benjamin to G. Scholem, June 12, 1938

—which doesn't mean that you can't transmit a little, the Tradition you only half hear, pass it on in bits and pieces—the defense of the truth, and of those who would extend it, even by evading it; the opposition to war and the devotion to peace; the styles of elegance and expertise in art and science; the beauty of the plain and simple (and the cryptic and the complicated); the methods for coping with the unbearable, and caring for that which makes it less so; the ways of loving what is, and laboring to bring about what should be.

My mom likes to tell the story about how once, when she and my dad were first married (this must have been sometime during the second Eisenhower administration), they were out somewhere in the woods with some other newlyweds, staying in some kind of log cabin (somewhere in eastern Washington State, I suppose—I can't recall the details) without electricity or running water. One morning, my dad came back from the well with an empty bucket. ("Your father didn't know anything about priming the pump!" my mother reports with gleeful and affectionate condescension.) Well, as little as he knew, I know less, and my ears glaze over whenever my mother seeks to explain with methodical clarity the practice and principle of this hydraulic feat for drawing water where all seems dry. I have never delved to consider the literal ground of what is best known as a popularizing metaphor for a central element of Keynesian economics, and certainly have no interest in disturbing the perfect record of my ignorance.

But I like to think about how much my mother likes to tell me all about it.

Note: "(a sort of theology passed on by whispers dealing with matters discredited and obsolete)" (Benjamin to Scholem).

3303. Notes toward Aphorisms

> Above all, Bacon gave him an ideal of style involving a union of compression and metaphor, of practical wisdom and imagination. … "Their excellence and value," Reynolds quotes him as saying, "consisted in being the observations of *a strong mind operating upon life*."
>
> W. Jackson Bate, *Samuel Johnson*

I used to think that strength would always be the property of the *other* party. It was *life* and its operators that seemed strong, and you and I no more than their prolix and played-upon players. Lately, though, I've been feeling pretty strong myself, watching for when to make my move and make my mark. You never know when your call will come to rise and shine (accidents of lucidity and love; surprises of séance and sentence), nor how long (except, not long) your time in the light will last (house rules, and always wins in the end).

Our better oracles say that the strongest speech (as with the sweetest) may be short: though uneasy, you turn to face the music, before it drowns you out.

We poor players know to seek to make our cake-walk better, even by the fast firework, the *brief candle*, that comes right before the Dark.

Note: "Beauty is as summer fruits, which are easy to corrupt, and cannot last … but yet certainly again, if it light well, it maketh virtue shine, and vices blush" (Bacon, "Of Beauty").

MARCH 2012

3313. “Money is a kind of poetry”

Wallace Stevens

Yesterday, after my annual visit, I left my accountant’s office with tears in my eyes. I don’t think I’ve ever left my accountant’s office actually weeping. Maybe I have and just forgotten. I cry a lot, and I have a terrible memory.

Once a year, I see him about my taxes. My brother thinks I’m wasting my money. I think I’m saving my soul. Also, a lot of time and peace of mind: I’m terrible with numbers.

Especially numbers that are symbols for money. Or maybe those numbers are bad with me—hell, either way, it’s an ugly relationship, and I’ve basically given up on it. (Don’t tell *them* that—the numbers, I mean: they know *exactly* where I live, and they’ll come after me six ways to Sunday.)

On the other hand, like you, I hope, I’m involved in a lot of relationships—close encounters, lifelong romances, or something simpler (like a good neighbor)—that just get better every year. With each passing year, for example, my appreciation for the kinds of words that help people get through a dark night or a long day just grows and grows. With each passing year, the kinds of words that help people get brave or loving, or help them know that they can become so—their interest compounds like nobody’s business.

Appreciating words like that, and helping others do so, too: well, that’s the better part of my business. Of course, I lack the instruments to quantify the rescuing resonances of the kinds of words that are the stock in trade for retail outfits like mine—like I say, unlike my accountant, I'm not a numbers man. But let me tell you something: every year, I leave his office a little less worried than I was when I walked in, and numbers or no numbers, I have to figure that the better part of both our businesses is pretty much the same.

Note: "All these forms, familiar to all the arts, place us at a distance from the substance of things; they speak to us 'as from afar'; reality is touched not with direct confidence but with fingertips that are immediately withdrawn" (Georg Simmel, *The Philosophy of Money*).

3314. We Apologize for the Allusions

> The quotations, direct or indirect, that figure so prominently … Some readers … regard their presence as an affectation, even a pedantry. A sympathetic view might take them as additional "voices" that haunt the poem, or the poet's mind in his making of the poem.
>
> Lionel Trilling on "The Waste Land," *The Experience of Literature: A Reader with Commentaries*

Sometimes I think maybe it's just because poets, like people in general, get lonely now and then, and want to have as many friends as possible around them, as they make their way through whatever fear or favor they happen to be facing any given day or night. You lose so many friends as the years go on (a loss of life; a failure of love; a misplaced address)—it's hard to keep in mind that those you have left don't necessarily all know each other; so that the unannounced return of an old one from twilight sleep or fervid youth gets you so excited—*an abstract idea, a painting, stippled Hopkins or shorn Baudelaire, God or Shakespeare* (Nabokov, *Lolita*)—that you forget your manners and neglect to present him properly to the others in the room. Maybe you think they already know each other. (They often do: when I was in college, I was forever introducing people to one another who had known each other well before they had known me—*how embarrassing*.)

Sometimes I think all those *quotations, direct or indirect, that figure so prominently* are just so many well-meaning networkers, working really late—long past the due date—like the exercise of a phantom limb that would if it could (but it can't) rescue a failed cry for help:

> "Don't let him cut my hand off—
> The doctor, when he comes. Don't let him, sister!"
> So. But the hand was gone already.
> (Robert Frost, "Out, Out—")

(I always wished I'd done more to help out my brother and sister during their Hard Times.)

Anyway, it's about old friends (*When Harry Met Sally*).

Note: "The author and annotator of the 'piece that passeth understanding' was not insensitive to the resulting climate of jest. Six years later he capped a comparison between Crashaw and Shelley by calling for elucidation of the 'Keen as are the arrows' stanza of 'To a Skylark': 'There may be some clue for persons more learned than I; but Shelley should have provided notes'" (Hugh Kenner, *T. S. Eliot: The Invisible Poet*).

3317. "a preponderance of loving affections"

> In re-reading my manuscript, I am almost appalled
> at the amount of emotionality which I find in it.
>
> William James, *The Varieties of Religious Experience*

Really? Now see, re-reading *my* manuscript, I would have felt that I had failed its subject (the subject being you and me, and all that we've been through together ... or, if not together, still near enough one another, and surely never, quite, without each other), if the emotional amount had been any *less*.

Note: "God only knows what I'd be without you" (Beach Boys, "God Only Knows").

3871. Conversion for Dummies

Much like my mother, Edward Gibbon sharply disapproves of "opulent nobles" who "resign ... their leisure to the business and amusements of private life" (*Decline and Fall of the Roman Empire*) rather than joining the PTA, a political cause, or "the pursuit of military glory." Not least amongst the downsides of what both deem so much selfish self-indulgence is its vitiating effect on the body and mind of those so indulgent:

> Should a fly presume to settle on the silken folds of their gilded umbrellas, should a sunbeam penetrate through some unguarded and imperceptible chink, they deplore their intolerable hardships, and lament in affected language that they were not born in the land of the Cimmerians, the regions of eternal darkness. (Gibbon, *Decline and Fall*)

The pattern of decadence that Gibbon sets forth here strikes a little too close for comfort, *para mí*. While I have little concern for the perfected imperviousness of silken folds or gilded umbrellas, I decline and fall to the Dark Side at the very prospect that I might be deprived, for an epoch or an hour, of the less ostentatious, but surely no more admirable, armoring ornaments of argument by which I make my way through this world.

What happens when the sheltering, glittering certitudes that make me feel safe and Proud turn into so many bare, ruined choirs, repeating the same old slogans, like so many veterans of the Boer, and other, wars?

I guess then it's time for keener-sounding adventure; a newer course of study.

Note: "The anxiety in teaching, in serious communication, is that I myself require education. And for grownups this is not natural growth, but *change*. Conversion is a turning of our natural reactions; so it is symbolized as rebirth" (Stanley Cavell, *The Claim of Reason: Wittgenstein, Skepticism, Morality, and Tragedy*).

4004. "a love stronger than any impulse that could have marred it"

> She never repented that she had given up position and fortune to marry Will Ladislaw. … They were bound to each other by a love stronger than any impulse which could have marred it.
>
> George Eliot, *Middlemarch*

My mother likes to remind me regularly of her aversion to fiction and, in particular, the kind of "fancy" fiction I have spent a good portion of my life studying and teaching. I was thus surprised this morning, in my semi-annual survey of her strange library—manuals for Hikers, Self-Helpers, and Chinese Communists; a celebratory biography of Andrew Jackson; memoirs of Native American Warriors and dictionaries of Ancient Hawaiian Chants; histories of the Middle East and the Wild West; old (very old) field guides to flora and fauna, near and far; textbooks on Organic Chemistry and the like—to discover, nearly hidden in the thickets of this old curiosity shop, one of "my" books—a novel I am not alone in regarding as one of the greatest stories ever told. More surprising, still: the volume is, throughout, underlined and annotated by what could only be her hand.

I was less surprised to discover that amongst the passages she has marked for note are the lines that begin this report. Decades after their divorce, my parents remain bound together by an unfaded, though now hardly mentioned, belief that risking anything short of everything to marry each other (they are of different races; that was a different time) would have been a cowardice they would have both repented till the day they died. I like to think that my mother took some satisfaction when she came across a bare statement of the fact of the faith that determined the direction of her life—"a feeling that,

---

Note: in gaining the man she loved, she would gain something for the whole world" (E. M. Forster, *A Room with a View*).

4010. "a piece of classical debris which insists on being noticed"

Maurice Natanson, *Edmund Husserl: Philosopher of Infinite Tasks*

God, what isn't? I mean, what isn't *a piece of classical debris which insists on being noticed*? What is the first worry in the morning but a fragment of the oldest fear (fear itself) in the book—that book, as drowned now as any secret of the deep? What is the feeling of defeat, before the infinite tasks of the day have even begun, but a torn passage from a poem of a being at a loss, written in sentences too old and cold now for anyone to parse? What is the sense that you're past all help (giving or getting), but the repeating story of exile whose hidden foundation evades all excavation?

What is the push to love past all our woe but the renewal of vows voiced, for the first time, before all our first times? What is the reaching and being reached that starts the movement of any calmness and kindness but offspring of the first mothered gesture of every better nature? What is the starting transmission that tells you *you've got this*, but a sending as old as a sword from a stone, an easing that comes from a classic *you love*?

90

Note: "Many of their ideas are merely a matter of historical curiosity, but some of them contain a nucleus of permanent truth and might thus become a message and an inspiration … to the rest of mankind" (Paul Oskar Kristeller, *Renaissance Thought: The Classic, Scholastic, and Humanist Strains*).

APRIL 2012

4014. "cleaning house and throwing out things you know you're going to miss"

> It's like cleaning house and throwing out things you know you're going to miss—there comes a time when junk dreams get in your way.
>
> Pauline Kael, reviewing *The Long Goodbye*

And you just know you're going to miss them all—all that *junk:* especially when they are the sum total of all that remains of the few you had felt by the beat of your heart you just couldn't ever do without; and knew in the back of your mind had basically left the building about as soon as they had come. ("The lover's anxiety: ... the fear of a mourning which has already occurred, at the very origin of love." Roland Barthes, *A Lover's Discourse: Fragments*)

Anyway, you've only got so much space at the place where you really live, and you just know that if you want to make room for more company, you have some serious housecleaning to do. You just know (as much as you hate zero sums), to let in a new round of comings and goings, you need to toss out souvenirs of old ones. You just know that

---

Note: "Life is the elimination of what is dead" (Wallace Stevens).

4020. "Why Write?" (Sartre)

> ... breaking a wounded silence ... in companionable talk ... the conversation that helps, in trouble; balm to hurt minds ...
>
> Denis Donoghue on Randall Jarrell, "The Lost World"

All those face-to-face conversations that you meant or mean to have, but can't, now—not yet, anyway; or not anymore, maybe: frank and forgiving, face-to-face conversations, whose time is passed or, perhaps, to come. You don't know whether it's too early or too late for them, and maybe the best you can do unless and until you do is some essay that would "steer a middle course" between requiem and rehearsal for the prime-time sound stage of voices mingling; "a middle course" between a "style ... familiar" (Hazlitt, "On Familiar Style") enough to recall the signature sounding of someone you've loved; and foreign enough to release someone you might love even more.

Note: "Balm of hurt minds, great nature's second course" (Shakespeare, *Macbeth*).

4021. Principia Mathematica

> Like an object whose loss has begun to be felt ...
>
> John Ashbery, "Lost and Found and Lost Again"

—like the light of a world that someone you love, try as he might, could never pass on to you.

When I was a boy, my father labored by the light of the best of his love to teach me what he knew about what could be known, and what never known. Principles of Uncertainty and Prisoner's Dilemmas—I only pretended to understand the basic math that underwrote and animated his conscientious labors to convey all he knew (and knew that he didn't) to me. I'm pretty sure he knew in the back of his mind that I was faking it.

Here's what I know I surely know I will never know: would it console him to know that since my graduation from his home-school of geometry, out here on my own, I've learned a little about principles of uncertainty and prisoner's dilemmas, even without the math? Would it console him to know that I wish I could show him my work?

Note: "The teaching of Divine truth must still be a mystery" (Ruskin, *Modern Painters*, part 2, section 6, chapter 2).

4023. "how to talk to people you don't like"

> "Neither you nor Buddy know how to talk to people you don't like." She thought it over. "Don't love, really," she amended.
>
> J. D. Salinger, *Franny and Zooey*

And what makes matters worse, I often think that I *do* when I *don't*. I often think that I know *just* how to converse with people dwelling on the dry side of indifference; how to talk them and me *both* into thinking that I *really do* like them, even really, *really love* them (and thus—*full* disclosure—*they, me*). But it's all an enchanted forest, a bare and barely demilitarized zone of so many *pretty* lies—or, no better, half-truths; so many sentences with too many stress marks, and too little chance for what is best left undervoiced.

But things are looking up, I like to think. I like to think that somehow in the midst of a lifelong chattering, charm offensive, whether through those silent spaces that come between the panzer paragraphs of my prolixity, where people are able to get a word in, edgewise (those spaces get bigger with age: the Old-School, Mobile Army of Metaphors, having mostly run on nonrenewable, Nietzschean energy ever since it first got mechanized, is getting a little exhausted), or a corresponding refinement of curiosity about what that Child-Wise, Edge word might be, or might become, if it is allowed room enough to grow up, I've learned a little about how you might end up liking, even loving, people you weren't expecting to feel much for when the peace talks started (when it came time for those talks, it used to be that I'd always look to run the clock out—gaming the shape of the negotiating table, or by some other cute trick of the filibuster).

What I've learned about really liking and loving people on the other side of the Table Talk is pretty simple, actually. I'm sure you knew it already. (All these years, I've prided myself on being a quick study; turns out, when it comes down to a lot of the things that matter most, I'm a pretty slow learner.)

How do you talk to people you don't like or love, so that you give all parties involved a decent chance of finding some grace-noting, new-sounding light at the end of the Tunnel?

Easy. You don't talk. You listen.

Note: "dial tone, of course, followed the formal break in the connection. She appeared to find it extraordinarily beautiful to listen to, rather as if it were the best possible substitute for the primordial silence itself … all of what little or much wisdom there is in the world" (Salinger, *Franny and Zooey*).

4037. "aspects of the life of Jack Kennedy of which Lyndon Johnson was unaware"

> There were … aspects of the life of Jack Kennedy of which Lyndon Johnson was unaware. … Behind that easy, charming, carefree smile on the face of the ambassador's second son was a life filled with pain.
>
> Robert Caro, *The Years of Lyndon Johnson: The Passage to Power*

Well, you can hardly impeach him for *that:* powers of discernment far above and beyond even those attached to LBJ's outlandishly off-scale pay grade at the Department of Human Fallibility would have been demanded to deduce, at the time, the deep and daily physical anguish that defined his second most salient rival's every move and motion. Not even that most practiced and talented marker of human weakness and woe (this side, anyway, of Olympus or Sinai) could be expected to penetrate the vast fleet of many-winged conspiracies that worked their craft day and night to keep up the appearances of all that glamorous vivacity and vigor; to make his way past all that and gather near the body just on the other side of the curtain; the body ever in pain; the body that, long before Dallas, lay ever near dying.

After all, as we all well know, even imagining the pain of our nearest neighbors, that "element of tragedy which lies in the very fact of frequency" (Eliot, *Middlemarch: A Study of Provincial Life*)—even the most elementary approximations of pain (*I may know that he is in pain, but I never know the exact degree of his pain* [Wittgenstein])—involve acts and attitudes of patience and perception that surpass our understanding:

> Pain has an element of blank;
> It cannot recollect
> When it began, or if there were
> A day when it was not.
> (Emily Dickinson)

The Biography of Pain: some would call that God's Work. And some have held "that here on earth

---

Note: God's work must truly be our own" (John Kennedy, "Inaugural Address").

4039. "a cry of pure pain"

In the ... wild laughter of the book, there is a cry of pure pain.

Mary McCarthy on Nabokov's *Pale Fire*, "A Bolt from the Blue"

—and, lo and behold, it's brought to you by the *last* people you'd expect to hear it from; the last people you'd expect to carry the cracking sound of anguish close to your ears—both of them about as compassionate as a piece of dry ice sculpture (what a Piece of Work, the both of them!)—but listen, and you'll hear the pain they want you to hear. Just like how you can sometimes hear in the strain of a mean and snobby joke, someone lonely, wanting someone near; like how every once in a while you discover hidden in the most noisy exhibitionist ruse, a beaten heart's hapless and unheard appeal for some fair peace; like how, once in a blue moon, you come upon, in the broadcast self-confidence of pedant or pervert, the Confession of his knowledge that the one Authority from whom he seeks Sanctuary, never lets the Petitioner near his Premises in the first place ("Lady Augusta is the one character he could ever really imagine, partly no doubt, because she could not imagine *him*." Mary McCarthy on Oscar Wilde's *The Importance of Being Earnest*).

And then you remember: just because someone can't get out of her own dry head doesn't mean that she doesn't want you in her own deep heart.

Note: "I was mentally composing a telegram to the Pope" (Mary McCarthy, *The Seventeenth Degree: How It Went, Vietnam, Hanoi, Medina, Sons of the Morning*).

MAY 2012

4047. "Several people on the trip told me that I was an inspiration, which made me feel good" (The Author's Mother)

> And now you will no longer wonder that the recollection
> of this incident on the Acropolis should have troubled
> me so often since I myself have grown old and stand
> in need of forbearance and can travel no more.
>
> Freud, "A Disturbance of Memory on the Acropolis"

Many years ago, in the middle of the hardest defeat of my life, my mother came to visit me in New York. My apartment there is small; I, especially in my compromised state, smaller still, and my powers to accommodate her sizable stock of certitudes and self-doubts—their aggregate volume sufficient to fill any proscenium worth its salt—powers of forbearance that hardly amount to the armor of Hercules even in the best of times, reduced to the tattered thinness of a single fig leaf. *She couldn't have come at a worse time*, I thought—until I realized that she couldn't have come at a better one.

Seeing that I was in no shape to chaperone her, she struck out on her own. (She is, after all, according to her own Ancient History, of "pioneer stock.") One morning, she left before I was awake and called me later from the viewing platform at the top of what was then the City's tallest building, while I was still in bed. From this height, she felt called upon to tell me something about herself that she instructed me not to repeat, and I will not disobey her.

What I *can* tell you is that what she conveyed to me when I was troubled, and in need of forbearance, was a memory of falling down and getting up again that dissipated the disturbance that left me thinking I could travel no more.

And now I no longer wonder that my sorrow at the thought of the day that she will pass beyond me is matched by the strength with which she has prepared me to meet it.

Note: "The two days in Athens were great but tiring. I actually made all of the excursions (one exception: a Venetian castle in Crete, but went everywhere else). Some people did not climb up the Acropolis, but I did. Why come to Greece and not go up? Was worth it. I was glad that I had both walking sticks. It really made it possible. Several people on the trip told me that I was an inspiration, which made me feel good. I will tell you all more about the trip later, and show you the pictures when I get them done" (extracted from my mother's report on her most recent travels; her destination this time was the Mediterranean rather than Manhattan).

4050. "I think to myself: where have they gone?"

Alfred Kazin

Wait: *They were just here*—friends, neighbors, teammates, allies, opponents, friendly international competitors and collaborators (*they're friends, and they're foes too*—Joni Mitchell, "Trouble Child")—all those sullen and sudden types who stood between you and the Bar, or raised it beyond, to all Recognition. All those crowded conversations (free or freighted), come crashing through the night and there you are (wait: I mean, there you *were*), suddenly discovering *yet once more—one more round!*—the engrossing problem of other minds. (You thought you'd be together for the length of a couple of drinks or all of your decades, but he or she or they, or the destiny enfolding each and every one of us, had other plans. *Destiny stands by sarcastic with our dramatis personae folded in her hand* [George Eliot].) Where are they now, all those wild things, all those quick, bright things? You knew even then, in the midst of the attracting, distracting swag and swagger, they'd all come to confusion, and you first of all.

Still, though, dizzy as I get just thinking about all those ridiculously *dizzy raptures*, now mostly faded *into the light of common day*—I just know, *lonely as a cloud* as I guess I like to be now, (Wordsworth), as high and dry as my Ice Age demands I be now (dryer, and way less dirty than any martini I ever saw back, as they say, in the day), still though, I'm pretty sure, still: *I could drink a case of you* and

---

Note:

Still I'd be on my feet
I would still be on my feet.
(Joni Mitchell, "A Case of You")

4060. Noncomputable Memories

Like countless others in the digital age, I seem
To have written a memoir on my new computer.
It had no memories—anyone's would have done,
And mine, I hoped, were as good as anyone's.

James Merrill, "Scrapping the Computer"

My mother is wary of these machines. She worries that they coax us to confess at least a little more than we normally would, and a little more than we ever should—like a crafty analyst or crafted analog, or one of those calculating characters from weird novels or nights, who get more tears out of and in you than you ever intended for them to get. I know she's right (she pretty much always is), but here's the thing: if, as I hope, my memories are as good as anyone else's, I'm also fairly sure that they're no worse than anyone else's, either. And even in the worst-case scenarios (all those ancient and modern histories of anguish, too dark to describe in detail or heal in whole), you try to keep on course, and patch together something better out of something seriously bad—like when Hepburn cheers Bogart on as he hauls their failing craft (*The African Queen*) through the last swamp, quietly knowing quite well that they're quite doomed, and quietly knowing that he quite knows it too.

Note: "Perfectibility and the associated idea of equality ... he was keen to reaffirm" (Etienne Hofmann, "The Theory of the Perfectibility of the Human Race," *The Cambridge Companion to Benjamin Constant*).

4063. "Things answer only if they are questioned"

> Things answer only if they are questioned, and ... we cannot overlook the fact that in their emergence ... answers are systematically conditioned ... through their bond to the question.
>
> Erwin Straus, *Event and Experience*

Except, it seems, when you're dreaming, and then everything (you included) appears to be nothing *but* answers, no questions asked. And the answers (*mutatis mutandis*) always more or less amount to the same one: *Yes, I miss you more than I can bear.*

What a relief, when we rouse ourselves and get ourselves together and shake ourselves apart, and, settling down to "[our] books or [our] business" (Thackeray), start to see that

---

Note: "the thing we freely fórfeit is kept with fonder a care" (Hopkins, "The Leaden Echo and the Golden Echo").

JUNE 2012

4073. Helping a Stranger Feel at Home

> Pope very nearly succeeded in doing the impossible, in naturalizing an alien literary tradition and form.
>
> Reuben A. Brower, *Alexander Pope: The Poetry of Allusion*

It's the love that you show by how you construe, for someone from somewhere else, the feeling of being at home. It's the respect that you show by admitting you know that she never really, fully will.

Note:

Color of context, imperceptibly
Rustling with its angel
(James Merrill, "Lost in Translation")

4081. "In the vast literature of love"

> John Updike

there has never been, nor will be, a love quite like ours. That's what all of the literature of love believes. Otherwise it wouldn't be vast. Otherwise it wouldn't be love.

Note: “Love you, man” (sentence abbreviated).

4094. “She touched—she admitted—she acknowledged the whole truth”

Jane Austen, *Emma*

Those of us happy to call ourselves her friends will scarcely be surprised by the unstinting intellectual availability that marks our heroine’s brightest days. Such open-mindedness is, after all, part and parcel of the hospitality well bred into her being.

Welcome, she will say to all who visit her at Hartfield (you know: where she lives) as she touches, admits, and acknowledges as much of them as she feasibly can.

Those who talk too much. Those who talk too little.

Those special deliverers who arrive unannounced, out of nowhere you can see; and, bypassing the usual set-pieces of parlor-room settlements, proceed straight to her heart, with breakthrough news, straight from the underside of the field of her heart.

“It darted through her with the speed of an arrow, that”

Note: “we never discover a ‘no’ in the unconscious” (Austen, *Emma*; Freud, “Negation”).

speed of an arrow; force of the id

4098. "To wait"

O ecstatic
Receiver of what's there to be received,
How we belabor thee, how much better
To wait and to prepare our waiting

John Ashbery, "Becalmed on Strange Waters"

In your frenzy for the results of that test (sickness or health; life or death; up or down; love or loss), you can sometimes forget that you're never waiting alone. There's always at least one other person in the room who needs to be calmed more than you do: the Frenzied Receiver, sitting there, just on the edge of yourself, on edge; as near to you as anyone you've ever loved could ever possibly be; the Frightened Receiver, with whom you are so closely crowded together that it's easy to confuse her with your own ache; overlook her as nothing more than more of your own ache (hard not to, what with all the overlap of one with the other—the genetic, generic material you share); the Fearful Receiver, for whom you rouse yourself from the stupor of your sole self, to address with whatever compassion and courage you have at your command to convey.

And then, *look!*, it's the two of you, together—and there's room to breathe, room to wait,

---

Note: "world enough and time" (Marvell).

4100. The Near Enough Angel

> The presence or countenance of the beloved one—whom he was resolved never to leave even though he did not possess her … the angel … [upon] whom [Benjamin] … casts his wide-open eyes … like the melancholy view that discovers … the infinite depths of allegories, without however being able to complete the step over the transitory into the religious sphere …
>
> Gershom Scholem, "Walter Benjamin and His Angel"

—which brings me to Fernando Torres. Now, I'm as certain as I am of anything under the sun that Young Torres has only the vaguest idea that I'm alive. There is little reason for me to believe that a somewhat shy-seeming Spanish Striker, playing, however uneasily, on the brightly lit field of international celebrity, knows or cares about me, personally.

I can live with that. Why should he, really? Although I entertain my share of outlandish ambitions, I do not count amongst them the desire to annex, as my own, the attention of a distant Star; even one whose remote influence has tided me over my darkest nights and granted me title to my brightest days. The lunacy of my greed has not, at least last I checked, thus far extended that far.

Here's something else I can live with: truth is, just as I'm pretty sure he doesn't know much about me, I really don't know much about him. That is, I don't know what he's like in real life, and I have never been especially concerned to find out. Give the man his space—that's what I say. Also, I've never been especially interested in figuring out, with the help of this or that mythological, methodical key of comprehension, any bright, particularly distinct, defining quality and destiny, situated in some heavenly abstraction, beyond the trapping feelings of everyday life, to which such a Star would show me the way.

I'm just really grateful he's around—the kid, I mean: the Spanish Striker. Catching sight of him in the midst of his beautiful game, all I care to think is

---

Note: "He comes to save" (John Henry Newman, "Consolation").

Allegory of Love—"wild emotional loyalty" (Walter Ong, SJ).

JULY 2012

4102. The Abstraction of Love

> What … is love, except a certain life which couples
> or seeks to couple together some two things, namely,
> him that loves, and that which is loved?
>
> Augustine, *On the Trinity*

That pretty much nails it, as far as I can tell. I can't think of much else love might be—except, sometimes, when it's a cloudy, uncertain life that knows to cherish the communion for which it stands and falls, by raising up to recognize some distance (long or short; temporary or terminal) between the parties it aims to connect.

As everyone knows, sometimes absence makes the heart grow the fonder; sometimes

---

Note: "Absence Makes the Heart" (Lynne Tillman).

4107. Sentiment and Author, Uncertain

> That passed over, this can too …
>
> "Deor," translated from the Anglo-Saxon by Seamus Heaney

A sight-slighting swelling surrounds an Island of Love or Loneliness; Glory or Gall: the inmate, his vision cut down to the set margin of seeing, just past his solitude, will wonder how long his sentence there will last.

He yearns for the line of his sight to end with a period. He hopes that the end of the line has point enough to stop, full, and old, and start a new season—but it could be the dash of the hope for something different—only the broken tiding of repeating waves.

How will he know? The line extends so far beyond the seeing powers of his parsing. He must trust the translation; hope that it's sound.

Note: Fred C. Robinson, "Lexicography and Literary Criticism: A Caveat," in James L. Rosier, ed., *Philological Essays: Studies in Old and Middle English Language and Literature in Honour of Herbert Dean Meritt* (The Hague: Mouton, 1970), 99–110.

"That passed over, this can too" ("Deor," trans. Seamus Heaney).

4112. The Trouble with Parting

> "Don't be sorry," said Dorothea, in her clear tender tones, "I would rather share all the trouble of our parting."
>
> George Eliot, *Middlemarch*

—which just goes to show that she would rather not part at all, since the real troubles of parting begin when you're too far apart to share them.

But then we hear *her clear tender tones*, the sound of her kindness reaching past the separation from what had once been the solid sense of a world you had held in common—and perhaps still do, or perhaps will one day again.

Note: "Darkling I listen" (Keats, "Ode to a Nightingale").

4113. "concealed from the reader"

In written literature both the author and his characters are concealed from the reader.

Northrop Frye, *Anatomy of Criticism*

—but not forever. The hunger for company sooner or later breaks through all the codes, ancient or modern, going or blocking its way.

Note: "Reader [...] [I] married him" (Brontë, *Jane Eyre*).

4118. The Mirror Stages

I grow old under an intensity
Of questioning looks.

"Mirror"

And then, reflecting back on those questioning looks, I grow curiously young again.

Note: "I walk through the long schoolroom questioning" (Yeats, "Among School Children").

4120. Beauty, Coming and Going

Beauty comes to life when she learns that her father needs her.

Bruno Bettelheim on "Beauty and the Beast," *The Uses of Enchantment: The Meaning and Importance of Fairy Tales*

Beauty comes to life when she learns that her father needs her—and Beauty's father, when that time has finally come, finely learns to leave her be.

Note:

grown unpresuming,
almost Japanese
(James Merrill, "Prose of Departure")

4129. "Turn your fear into a safeguard"

> Turn your fear into a safeguard. … We are not always in a state of strong emotion, and when we are calm we can use our memories and gradually change the bias of our fear, as we do our tastes. Take your fear as a safeguard. It is like quickness of hearing.
>
> George Eliot, *Daniel Deronda*

The man who says these things has no choice but to say them quickly, to a woman who has no chance (it's an emergency) if she cannot hear them just as quick. You and I, however we may feel in the middle of the night, are most likely a little luckier. Probably we are in no present danger (probably just the usual Dark-Side dread) and can thus ponder a little more leisurely, a little more lucidly, the instructions that must be delivered here in utmost haste. Perhaps we are calm and clear enough, even now, even in the midst of the pitch where our own wild things are, to begin to put into practice the plan passed on by a hurried messenger to a harried hearer. Perhaps we are already a bit disposed to try to change the bias of our fear into the basis of a broader safety; ready, willing, and able to start to sharpen what senses we need to guard what we know of "*every* human love" (Auden; stress added).

Note: "And this thy harbor, O my City" (Hart Crane, "The Tunnel," *The Bridge*).

4130. "and apply yourself to your books or your business"

> When you come home you sit down in a sober, contemplative, not uncharitable frame of mind, and apply yourself to your books or your business.
>
> Thackeray, *Vanity Fair*

—home from a terrible dream, a lot more harrowing than any life that you would ever lead now (that life would have destroyed you); home from departings, a little harder than you expected (what loss, worth its salt, isn't?); home to the plainer fortunes, the calmer fortress (your office, your skill-set, your sense that the mission you chose to accept is still true); home to the soft landing where you spend most of your waking hours, now—still ready to receive what's new.

Note:

> the reader leaned above the page,
> Wanted to lean
> (Wallace Stevens, "The House Was Quiet and the World Was Calm")

THE
VICTORIAN
FRAME OF
MIND, 1830-1870
Walter E. Houghton

4132. "I dwell with a strangely aching heart"

Robert Frost, "Ghost House"

—and, strange to say, the ache gets easier every day.

Note: "look in thy heart, and" (Sidney).

AUGUST 2012

116 4136. "the dread fear of the unemployed that the world needed them no longer"

> We were poor indeed, Roosevelt said, if this nation could not lift from every recess of American life the dread fear of the unemployed that the world needed them no longer.
>
> Arthur M. Schlesinger Jr., *The Politics of Upheaval*, vol. 3 of *The Age of Roosevelt*

When I was a boy, my family lived for a while near a small farm that we could see from our house (at least that's what I remember—it was probably further than that). One time, my father took me with him to buy corn from the man who made his living by working the farm. (He reminded my brother and me of "Mr. Green Jeans" from *Captain Kangaroo*.)

It couldn't have been much of a living. He wasn't exactly unemployed—I guess "underemployed" is the term we'd use now: whatever he was doing, it probably didn't amount to what anyone reading this would call a living wage for himself and his family. I probably didn't pay much heed to this at the time. What I did notice at the time was the neighborly and respectful way my father spoke to him, and then something my father said to me as we drove away: Jeff, I paid him more for the corn than I would have paid at the store, because he's poor, and he needs the money for his family.

I'm not sure which struck me more—the extra money (knowing my father, I can tell you it probably wasn't much), or the friendly respect he paid the farmer. But I'm pretty sure I understood that by my father's calculations (my father, unlike his first son, is good at math), the two things were on the plus side of the same equation.

4154. "the most surprising openness"

> [The Stranger] often receives the most surprising openness—confidences which sometimes have the character of a confessional and which would be carefully withheld from a more closely related person.
>
> Georg Simmel, "The Stranger"

—confidences called forth by the foolish foreigner, fumbling for the correct change (in currency, in custom, in conjugation). Confidences that sometimes have the character of a confessional—confessions of kindness, confessions those who have a lot in common to begin with are not disposed to make to one another. These confessions take various forms: the length of time the woman at the register will spend to show you the exact change required for the ice or the book you are trying to buy; the smile (not sinister) the soldier will flash at you (how peculiar you must seem to him, jogging by the high walls of the military headquarters he is charged with guarding); the countless rehearsals the bro at the bar will undertake with you to improve your pronunciation of the sounds of a language as strange to your tongue as they are mother to his.

I think that they must know something, these confessors of kindness. I think they must know that you are too new on the scene, too baffled, too blue in the face or the heart to attempt any show of knowing. I think they know that all you really want is to only connect (E. M. Forster).

Note: *Sólo quisiera dártela monda y desnuda, sin el ornato de prólogo, ni de la inumerabilidad y catálogo de los acostumbrados sonetos, epigramas y elogios que al principio de los libros suelen ponerse.* [My wish would be simply to present it to you plain and unadorned, without any embellishment of preface or uncountable muster of customary sonnets, epigrams, and eulogies, such as are commonly put at the beginning of books.] (Cervantes, *Don Quijote de la Mancha*)

118

4159. "the dimmer but yet eager Titanic life gazing and struggling on walls and ceilings"

> Ruins and basilicas, palaces and colossi, set in the midst of a sordid present, where all that was living and warm-blooded seemed sunk in … deep degeneracy; … the dimmer but yet eager Titanic life gazing and struggling on walls and ceilings …
>
> George Eliot, *Middlemarch*

It feels bad to want something badly: something well within sight but just out of reach. Of course, not to know, or remember knowing, this feeling brings on its own vexations. For those of us who dwell, just now, outside the State of such aching, frenzied, freezing yearning (having not yet known it, or having known it too well), the closer we are to the sight of it, the further we feel from the fact of it. For those of us who dwell, for now, outside this State, to see it up close is like watching a movie with the sound muted.

But then you remember that they used to somehow make movies without sound. And some of those movies were love stories, loud, somehow, with passionate regard. You may have seen one of those movies. Who knows, in your dreams or your own dark age, you may have been in one yourself. And who knows, maybe you'll actually be cast in one or another such moving picture, sometime, sooner or later, in a theater near you.

It could happen to you. Stranger things have happened. It's not like the age of miracles is ever really past.

Note: "that roar which lies on the other side of silence" (*Middlemarch*).

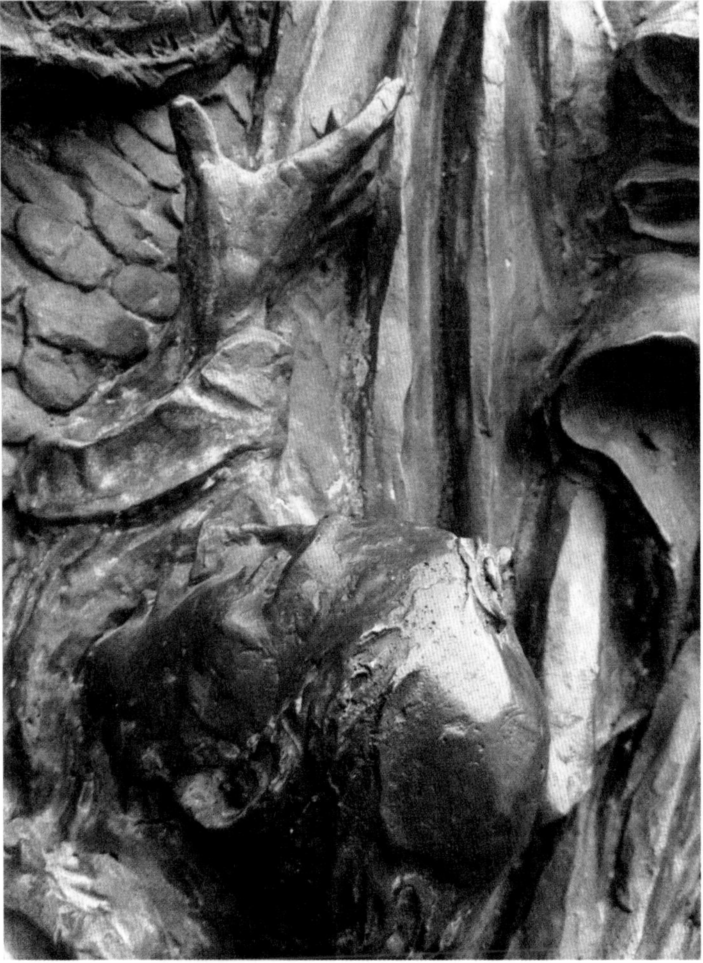

"They are leaning out for love . . . they will lean that way forever" (Leonard Cohen).

4161. Surpassing Speech

I am ashamed to admit that I am poor in languages that are not my own, and getting poorer all the time. While I do my best to converse in them, it's been years since I've gotten past primitive pleasantries and rudimentary requests.

Still, I love to be around them. Strange to say, the stumbling and solitary feeling that results from nearness to fluencies that will never be mine exhilarates as much as it exhausts and embarrasses me. For one thing, it's a little thrilling to be near the knowledge that you never really know most of what goes on between other people, and there's nothing like getting lost in a forest of alien idioms to force this knowledge on you.

And for another, when I am suddenly deprived of my facility for polishing my pressing feelings into punctilious speech, I am suddenly braced to remember how many yearnings are as dumb and dedicated as the foreigner who tries to speak a language well that he knows in his heart he never will.

Note:

The tumult in the heart
keeps asking questions.
(Elizabeth Bishop, "Conversation")

SEPTEMBER 2012

4170. "Good God, man, get on with your story!"

> Uncle Arthur ... never got through *Moby-Dick*, but how savagely he fought with Melville throughout the first fifty or a hundred pages! ... I discovered ... he had written in the margin ... "Good God, man, get on with your story!"
>
> Brendan Gill on Uncle Arthur, *Here at the New Yorker*

Though I sympathize with Uncle Arthur (who, having endured even while enjoying Melville, could help but share some of his impatience?), I think most of us are getting on (and along) with our story as best we can. What would help, of course, would be a better idea of what's going to happen in advance. Sure, there are plenty of clues (governing precedents, exigent circumstances, constitutional philosophies), but there's no expediting the outcome of determinations (dim or defined; casual or concentrated). At least there's no rushing the stories that do everything they can to make everyone think (themselves included) that, drowned or saved, they'll go on forever ... as long as they have a leg left to stand on, a bone still to heal, or the feeling that something's been forgotten, somewhere below what you see.

Note:

> The dice of drowned men's bones … bequeath
> An embassy (Hart Crane, "At Melville's Tomb").

"Sail on, sail on sailor" (The Beach Boys, "Sail on Sailor").

4172. Postseason Sentiment

> Only emotion endures.
>
> Ezra Pound, "The Art of Poetry"

Most times, it seems more like the opposite: more like only emotion perishes, while most everything else stays put. But even the most dug-out feeling persists, and knows what to do when it gets its turn at bat.

Making up for lost time, it'll knock you out of your park.

Note:

You can never tell with either
how it will go
or what you will do.
(Marianne Moore, "Baseball and Writing")

4181. "The voice reaching us from a great distance must find a place in the text"

> Different "heterologies" (sciences of the different) have the common characteristic of attempting to write the voice. The voice reaching us from a great distance must find a place in the text.
>
> Michel de Certeau, "Quotation of Voices"

Voices of people I have loved, or have wished that I could, carry themselves from far away, and make themselves at home in the nearby neighborhood of the books I like to read, coming to nest in this or that favorite piece of poetry or prose.

At least I think it's them. Maybe it's just me. Or maybe it's more like some harmony between us.

There was this girl I knew in college—I think it was college; maybe it was later; maybe before—I'm pretty sure I hear her (speaking or singing or crying) in most everything I care to read. On the other hand, I'm sentimental, and apt to exaggerate how much I recall of people that have meant a lot to me. Still, I'm pretty sure I hear her. She's gotten older and younger, more and less fluid and fragmented, but I'm pretty sure she's always there, her voice pressed into the words that matter to me most. It's like a story a friend told me once about how his grandmother, in her last years, heard the sound of the birds she'd grown up with singing in her ears everywhere she went. He says that he still remembers hearing the thrill in her voice when she first said something about it to him.

That may sound like a miracle. On the other hand, it's hard to imagine how you'd forget hearing something like that.

Note:

Never again would birds' song be the same.
And to do that to birds was why she came.
(Robert Frost, "Never Again Would Birds' Song Be the Same")

4182. Losing Voice to Regain It

She has an extremely soft, weak voice, as if she were afraid of losing it if she forced it a little.

Mircea Eliade, *Journal*, November 6, 1962

I wonder if she was right about the weakness of her voice. She probably wouldn't have lost it (not forever, anyway) if she had forced it a little, but what if she forced it a lot, and for a long time? I ask because sometimes when I'm feeling frayed or frustrated, and catch my voice sounding forced (fake), I suddenly fear that my whole being has been taken over by a Profane and foreign body that will rattle out false recordings across every distance, long and short, from here to eternity, thus casting the calls of Sincere and Sacred Sentiments into a limbo where they are forever waiting for their turn to be heard.

Later, after I give it a rest, it feels more real again. *Wow, that was a close call*, I think to myself.

Too close for comfort. Just close enough to wake me up so I can find some way to get some quiet and, after that, my true note.

Note: "… rest is silence" (Shakespeare, *Hamlet*).

“He’s off the hook for a while, quietly planning the Restoration of a Great Society—his silence ‘like Grant’s in Galena’” (F. Scott Fitzgerald, *Tender Is the Night*).

4183. “though now superseded in details”

On the general function of magic, a classic text, though now superseded in details, is Bronislaw Malinowski, *Magic, Science and Religion* (Boston, 1948). Malinowski calls magic “the specific art for specific ends.” ... “Magic is surrounded by strict conditions: exact remembrance of a spell, unimpeachable performance of a rite, unswerving adhesion to the taboos and observances which shackle the magician. If any of these is neglected, failure of magic follows.”

Angus Fletcher, “Allegorical Causation: Magic and Ritual Forms,” *Allegory: The Theory of a Symbolic Mode*, note 9

For about ten years, until about ten years ago, my running-mate and I would make the rounds most every weekend, on the lookout for a little magic we could call our own. Our preparations and our purposes were as routine as the coming of day (though they rather came at night, rather leaving with the coming of the day). Those wonder years have vanished for us now, replaced by new, more or less specific arts for new, more or less specific ends. I've been too busy accepting and articulating the mad methods of this latter-day magic to ask myself much whether I miss much the magic I've given up, and that's given up on me.

(It could be that the question never much comes up, because the one art and aim of this second, silver age of magic is remembering and revising the golden, gone one.)

All of this is old news, I know—a really small footnote to a really Big Story, studded with chapters like the one about how old magic rituals for getting what we want are modernized (turned into more scientific, experimental methods, subject to correction, reflection, and refinement), and the one about how all the new knowledge is always about all the old losses.

Speaking of experiments, I've been wondering a little lately about the ones that will light the way to the next age of magic. I'm hoping that it will be a little less about method and a little more about mystery; a little less about loss, and a little more about love.

Note: "an undecaying hope in our trivial ambitions" (Yeats, "The Moods").

4186. "the purpose of writing"

> The first piece of advice is this: to achieve style, begin by affecting none—that is, place yourself in the background. A careful and honest writer does not need to worry about style. As he becomes proficient in the use of language, his style will emerge, because he himself will emerge, and when that happens he will find it increasingly easy to break through the barriers that separate him from other minds and hearts—which is of course the purpose of writing, as well as its principal reward.

Strunk and White, *The Elements of Style*, 3rd ed.

I always know (always too late) when my words come too quickly and too loudly: too concerned about putting on a show to give other people in the room much of a chance to show a little themselves. What do I think I'm doing when I make this dumbfounding error, announced by the silence that succeeds my fast and furious words? I guess it's partly that I am prone to fall under the mistaken impression that I've been put in charge of Society—*I find it hard to divide myself into the executive me and me* (Howard Moss to Elizabeth Bishop). And I guess it's partly because I'm afraid that whoever's *really* in charge of Society (running the show, behind the scenes) will kick me out on my ass if I'm not singing for my supper, stylin as fast as I can, smack dab at the center of stage or page.

But the best elements of style are free. Compounded in ourselves, together they form whatever interest we have in really speaking to one another.

Note: "the purest, most transparent, and most casually appealing kind of interaction, *that among equals*" (G. Simmel, "Sociability as the Autonomous Form of Sociation").

4188. "their breathless disorder"

> Their breathless disorder, their passionate
> symbolism and their tone of prophetic preaching
> ... the appearance of a string of remarks.
>
> Sartre on Bataille, "A New Mystic"

Lately, I've been trying to improve the way I write: I've been trying to calm it down a little. Given all that's going on inside and outside where I live (maybe where you live, too), I'm not expecting miracles. I'll settle for a disorder that's a little less breathless; a prophetic tone a little less preachy. That's about as far as I plan on going right now. The swollen symbolism stays. Same with the string-theory remarks, as long and short, entwined and disentangled, as the strains of a lifetime. Like I say, there's too much going on, too much pressing down and pressing up for me to be trying Full On some Head-to-Toe, Plain Style. I'd be lying down on the job if I cut too much of the common-cloth chaos of duress and divinity that the work I try to do tries to distinguish, in some fashion. If I eliminated all the fast and fancy parts of speech, I'd lose too much of that. So I'm stuck with the *rapid flashes* (Bataille) that seeks to simulate what strikes at a speed that no clock can count; stuck writing the essay that tries with all its might *to include everything in a few sentences; anguish, decision* (Bataille).

Still though, even with all that's been and being thrown at us—*in a word, something* happened to *man* (Sartre)—even given all the givens—*too much grandeur in the human creature for us to understand him on the basis of his wretchedness, too much wretchedness for us to deduce his nature from his grandeur* (Sartre)—still, there's room for improvement (smoothing the temperature, while still feeling the tempest).

It's like the New Year's Resolution a friend made a few years ago: not to stop drinking, but to stop getting so messed up that she'd forget the morning after how she'd gotten home the night before.

Note: Letter to an Author:

> *Dear Mr. Levy:*
>
> *Thank you for your letter about* The Elements of Style. *I am glad you find it a good guidebook.*
>
> *I think that the expression "dress up" is a useful—certainly familiar—colloquialism. Little girls dress* up *when they go to a party, perhaps because their thoughts go upward. …*
>
> *Sincerely,*
> *E. B. White*

4189. Gods and Men

> Homer having made the Gods into men,
> man learned to know himself.
>
> M. I. Finley, *The World of Odysseus*

And I guess the first thing he learned about himself was that he himself wasn't actually much of a God.

But he can still be pretty good. Just think of how much we can care for one another, and how much we like to tell stories about how people who came before us cared for one another, too.

Sometimes, people have the strangest ways of showing that they care—strange as the ways of any God anyone's ever told me about. Take my best friend. It seems like he's never around when I think I need him most.

And he's always right there when it turns out I really do.

Note: "*The Odyssey* is about a man who cared for his wife and wanted to rejoin her" (Robert Fitzgerald).

Conveyors change, but the care stays, just the same.

4190. A Will, Thus a Way

Dante: "I could guide you into depravity, but I'm
not sure I could lead either of us back out."

Frank O'Hara

—though I'm pretty sure that together, with a little teamwork, we can make our way up and out of whatever the Hell they call the Darkness where we happen to be stuck now and then. Depravity, Depression—whatever: it's too damn dark to make out the street name, and it wouldn't help even if I could, since—well, just *since*. Let's just leave it at that. For once, let's just leave well enough alone. *The important thing is that we have each other.* I know that sounds ridiculous, but I've got it on the best authority that Salvation is supposed to be a *Comedy*, so I think we should just go with that.

You don't mind driving, do you? I'll navigate. Oh, wait. *You* navigate. (I can't read maps, Google or otherwise, and GPS—please. Be real. It's all I can do to figure out how to make the frickin windows go up and down—and where was I, btw., when the decision came down to make all windows *electric*? Why is *that* a good idea? What if the car goes over a bridge or something: wouldn't it be a lot easier, in the unlikely event of a water landing in the River Styx or one of those other Swamps, to open one of those "Old School" windows you just *roll* the *frick* down? Power windows are for the weak, that's what *I* say, and in a state of submergence, pretty much the last thing you need. Also, aren't they a waste of energy and aren't we supposed to be conserving or something, to keep the world from going to Hell in a Handbasket? I'm no Engineer, but it doesn't take too much time in the E-Quad to figure out *that* much.

My head is frickin' filled with all these excellent points, but no one with the keys to the kingdom pays much attention to what I say. I'm pretty much exiled from the corridors of power, when it comes to car and other driving designs. Bummer.)

Anyhoo, how about this: Instead of pretending that I can contribute anything practical, why don't I just talk while you get us the Hell outta here? How about that? Does that work for you? I'll just go on and on incessantly; we'll call that whole audio portion a Poem, once we call it a Day (once, thanks to You, we see Daylight). Maybe it'll relax you while you drive and do all the rest of the heavy lifting. It's a perfect setup. In fact, it's a match made in Heaven! By the way, another side note: why do my boys tell me that "guys" don't use exclamation points? What's up with that!?!?!?!?!?!?!?!?!?!?!?!?!?!?!?!?!!?!?!??!?!?!?!?!?!?!!??!

And speaking of *up*—

Note: *E quindi uscimmo a riveder le stelle* (And thence we issued forth to see again the stars) (Dante, Canto XXXIV, "Inferno," *The Divine Comedy*, trans. C. S. Singleton).

OCTOBER 2012

4196. Beyond Display

> Not that the reader is to suppose in Southey a showy master of rhetoric and colloquial sword-play, seeking to strike and to dazzle by his brilliant hits and evasions. The very opposite is the truth. He seeks, indeed, to be effective, not for the sake of display, but as the readiest means of retreating from display, and the necessity for display.
>
> De Quincey, "Literary Reminiscences"

I wonder how much the desire to dazzle is actually a forgotten hunger for a calmer kind of human contact, simmered beyond recognition by the fear that no one really likes what's really raw. Some of the best times I have with you are when I'm really tired, and my whole fleet of rhetorical devices and other vessels for fancy flying pretty much grounded: those times when I just want to be with you, and I've got nothing to offer but that wanting to be with you; those times when all passion for show is spent, and you seem happy enough to see me even without the *finery or parade* (Jane Austen); when what swaggers and struts or otherwise acts all superb sits silent, on the sideline; those times when you seem content just to *take me as I am* (Joni Mitchell).

And then, once we're all grounded and good, *frantic ingenuity* (Donald Davie on G. M. Hopkins) all forgotten; well, then—it's yet once more *wheels up* time, big time (this time, real time) and—*whoa!*—it's like we're walking on air (not putting on airs)—

Note: “High there” (Gerard Manley Hopkins, “The Windhover”).

4198. “but yes, of course, I loved the ... evenings of New York”

> The very smell of New York ... tracks you down in the heart of the most harmonious and familiar towns, to remind you there is at least one place of deliverance in the world, where you ... can finally lose yourself forever.
>
> Camus, “The Rains of New York”

But yes, of course, I loved those nights I got lost in New York. If I hadn’t loved them so much, how could I have ever left them? How could I ever hope to find them again (in my dreams; under a different dispensation of dearness; at a different pace of passion) if I had lost myself forever in them?

I guess it’s like any town that gets too damn hot for you to stay. You have to get away for a while, for good, though its *mysterious royalty has scarcely begun to shine.* (Camus, “Herman Melville”)

It’s the only way to cherish the memory of those nights. It’s the only way you’ll ever find something close enough again.

I know that.

“But

Note: I would be lying if I said I didn’t miss that other life, I loved it so” (E. B. White, “Time Past, Time Future”).

4200. "Come live with me, and be my love"

Christopher Marlowe

Wow. That may be the craziest proposition I've ever heard in my life. I think it may be even more out there in some outer space than my youngest nephew's view of the universe. (His head has all kinds of unusual thoughts. It's like a stadium, filled beyond all capacity with angels and aliens.)

Come live with me, and be my love. Is he on drugs? Does the word *tomorrow* ring a bell? (He must think there's no tomorrow: no black forests of death, disenchantment, dismemberment, division, derision, delusion, and divorce, just beyond his green-shaded thoughts.)

Come live with me, and be my love. He's high, right? At this late date, does anyone sober have the moxie to move in on someone this way? It would be like looking in the rearview mirror, by the full light of day, and not flinching.

Come live with me, and be my love. Can you seriously imagine saying this seriously to *anyone*, *ever* (or ever again)?

I hope so.

Note: "all the pleasures prove" (Christopher Marlowe, "The Passionate Shepheard to His Love").

4230. Some Wounded Trees

The forests are filled with them, and they cry when they bleed. And though they cry in various languages—*quid miserum, Aenea, laceras* (Virgil)*; Perché mi schiante?* (Dante); *et cetera* (Ariosto, Tasso, Freud)—basically, these trees of tears all come down to the same root: *why do you hurt me?*, they ask of the man who tears them.

Not that life was so great before the tearing—I mean, having your body turned into a tree (especially, as is often the case, after it has been mangled) can't exactly be anybody's idea of good times, but at least you're still standing (even if a little swollen), and maybe, as early as later today, you'll even provide some comfort and joy for an overheated traveler. Even the names of certain trees sound the secret of soothing:

> "eucalyptus"
> (From the Greek, *well-hidden*)
> (James Merrill, "Last Mornings in California")

And if some mornings you wake up, feeling a little hollow and haunted; set up for the Fall; if some mornings you wake up feeling stilled and stunted and sort of bled out, just think of your colors (the ones that don't run)—*laved past bleeding* (James Merrill, "Last Mornings in California"). Then maybe you can move a little, and then maybe a lot, and then maybe a whole Lot—like an uprooted forest in some play, returning home in a trick against the odds, like the spring that follows from a fall; like the light of the sun passing over a cover of leaves—*we're moving, we're moving …*

Note:

I think that I shall never see
A poem lovely as a tree.
(Joyce Kilmer, "Trees")

4231. The Importance of Being Alone

To be free is often to be lonely.

Auden

—sometimes it feels like it's nothing, but. And you know what? I'm fine with that. Like other single people I know, I need a lot of freedom to maneuver. Personally, I don't mind being a little lonely. I don't know how else to travel light enough to get to the places I need to get to on time (places where I feel needed; places, old and new; destinations I never really know in advance—like a heartbeat or a heartbreak, the need is actualized as soon as it's announced).

There's probably something pretty selfish and sad at the center of this schedule, but what with all the flight changes and missed connections that all of us (single or otherwise engaged) have to deal with in order to touch down on time, I currently lack the leisure to sort all that out.

Meanwhile, we solitary players (I guess we're all solo for at least a leg or two of the itinerary) just have to hope that our friends have enough faith in us to feel that even when we're just phoning ourselves in, we're doing our best to do more.

Note: "to aery thinness beat" (Donne, "A Valediction: forbidding mourning").

4232. "She was never wholly admirable"

> Somehow it was her disaster—her disgrace. It was her punishment to see sink and disappear here a man, there a woman, in this profound darkness, and she forced to stand here in her evening dress. She had schemed; she had pilfered. She was never wholly admirable. She had wanted success.
>
> Virginia Woolf, *Mrs. Dalloway*

Forced by what force, I wonder? What is it that keeps us (some of us, at least) keeping on keeping up our appearances, even when sinking and disappearing, or just staying in bed, seem like perfectly preferable options? I guess because people expect to see us—expect their breakfast or our brightness, no matter how same-old, same-old, our sunny-side up. And I guess what that means is that the same susceptibility to Society that will keep some of us from ever being wholly admirable is the best chance the same some of us have of being at least a little admirable, as well.

Note: "It seems a shame not to throw a fried egg on that" (my Mother, one morning, last March).

4237. "Often, almost nightly"

> Often, almost nightly, throughout the spring of 1959, I had feared for my life. Solitude is the playfield of Satan. I cannot describe the depths of my loneliness and distress.
>
> Nabokov, *Pale Fire*

While I share certain features of the condition and conviction confessed by the speaker here—surely so at this shady hour—I am no less struck by the differences between his state of mind and my own. It is true that I, too, have been and, moreover, continue to be, "almost nightly" visited by concerns vis-à-vis my life—but, in my own case (as I have already implied), they were hardly confined to the spring of 1959. (I was the barest of infants in the spring of 1959, little more than six months old, and while it is perfectly possible that I entertained fears about my life at that point in time, I remember them no better than I do the waning days of the Eisenhower administration, during which they would have occurred, if indeed they did occur.) Moreover and more importantly, in my own case, these nocturnal fears are rather more fears *of* my life than fears *for* it. (Make of these distinctions what you will: I am cogitating at the speed of flight, here, and cannot destroy my momentum with explanation.) And while I join the speaker in his conception of solitude generally, and especially that species of solitude that comes during the dead of night, as a kind of *playfield*, I have, in recent years, grown a little more inclined to survey that playfield as something a bit more felicitous and a bit less frightening: grounds populated by metaphorical jungle gyms and swing sets and seesaws and the like, ever present perhaps, but too oft overshadowed by schoolyard bullying evil and its baffling mirrors (Adorno: *in fascism the nightmare of childhood has come true*); too often bedeviled by unhappiness and its infinite apparatus. Finally, unlike the speaker, I am not aware of any difficulty describing the depths of my loneliness and distress. *That* I can spell out in my sleep.

On the other hand, you have to be pretty wide awake to parse out the grammar of ascent by which you figure your way out of them.

Note: “My aim is not to demystify myself, which would bore others and cause me despair” (Harold Bloom, “The Breaking of Form,” *Deconstruction and Criticism*).

4244. Bringing up Baby

Nick (*very quietly*): I think I understand this.
George (*ibid*): Do you?

Edward Albee, *Who's Afraid of Virginia Woolf?*

No, actually. He doesn't understand this. Oh, of course he gets the obvious play—an aged in woe, liquor-covered, wicked-funny couple (utterly witty, much as Macbeth and his Lady were upwardly mobile) make up a child to love as their own.

What he *doesn't* understand is what really happens once you really get started pretending that there are kids around you who are sort of your own: if you're in Earnest; if you make believe right, you really do bring a new person into the equation.

That person is you.

Note: "For unto us a Child is born" (Isaiah 9:6).

NOVEMBER 2012

4245. This Side of the Dark Side

> The conscious person is continuous with a wider self through which saving experiences come.
>
> William James, *The Varieties of Religious Experience*

November 1, 2012, at 3:18am

What happens in Vegas may stay in Vegas, but lately I've been thinking that the only games worth playing are the ones where what you lose and what you gain can spread some savings across state lines; spread into counties of consciousness; spread a little wealth there, at least a little further than any eye can foresee.

Note: "All my pretty ones" (Shakespeare, *Macbeth*).

4251. Can You Hear Me Now?

Sweet words are like honey: a little may refresh,
but too much gluts the stomach.

Anne Bradstreet

But how much is too much?—that's *my* question. I tend to err on the side of Excess: I know I talk too much, especially when I'm not sure about the reception. And lately, I've noticed, I can't figure out how and from where I receive half the things I say.

All I know is that I feel like I get a lot of calls that need to be returned or relayed.

And I've gotten mostly okay with that—mostly okay with all these comings and goings having their way through me, on their way to you.

I guess one mood's hopeless media is another mood's hope to meet.

Note:

If this
Be but a vain belief, yet … How oft, in spirit, have I turned to thee (Wordsworth, "Tintern Abbey").

4255. Weaker and Wiser

> She loves shocking stories: she has that coarse streak that usually goes with natures that are both fine and big. She wants people to like her, but if they do not it never worries or changes her.
>
> F. Scott Fitzgerald, *This Side of Paradise*

Often I wake in the dark to the thought of things I wish I hadn't said: the thought of someone shocked into silence, rather than brought to his senses. By the light of this dark, my coarse streak looks a mile wide and nowhere near fine: only an addicted, addled, roundabout garrulousness that can't resist the temptation of taking up too much space with too many hurled, hurtling syllables.

I lie in the dark and worry that people I like or wish I liked have come to dislike me, and for good reason, given all the things I've said.

This worry (older and younger than me, I know; older and younger than any Stop or Street I've known) has changed me some over the years. I hope it has changed me for the better and not for the worse.

Either way, it's morning now, light enough for anyone this tattered side of paradise to start looking for ways to bind together what words have drawn apart.

Note: "Life only avails, not the having lived" (Emerson, "Nature").

4258. The Care and Loving of a Gift

> "She's folded up in silver paper, you see, as if she was wrapped from head to foot in new Bank notes. Take care of her, and there's my hand, and thank you again."
> "I'll take more care of her than if she was a gold image," said Sloppy, "and there's both *my* hands, Miss, and I'll soon come back again."
>
> Dickens, *Our Mutual Friend*

They march along or move within you, but they never really shed their silver wrapping. No matter how much you lay your hands on them, you never really get the best gifts that you get. You lose them all the time (their movements are a mystery to you; they tend to go off on their own), but soon enough they make their way back to you again—one way or another. (Even my disastrous losses—a sterling-silver token of Adlai Stevenson's campaign, given by a Loyalist, and stolen from my mother's house; Welsh love spoons from the collection of a curious, dead uncle of someone I was once with, complete with an inscription no one will ever read—come back to me in dreams.)

If that's not an allegory for the best reunion ever, I don't know what is.

Note: "Such things please us best which are most strange, and come farthest off" (Robert Burton, *The Anatomy of Melancholy*; qtd. by Angus Fletcher, *Allegory: The Theory of a Symbolic Mode*).

4260. "your whole peculiar plot"

> The self and the earth—your thoughts, your feelings,
> Your beliefs and disbeliefs, your whole peculiar plot
>
> Wallace Stevens, "An Old Man Asleep"

Half asleep and halfway old, your whole peculiar plot starts to halfway write itself. That's when you halfway know that it's not really whole and not only yours.

Note: "I wanted to speak to you here, of the nature of these 'intellectual poems'" (György Lukács, "On the Nature and Form of the Essay").

4261. "What is truth?"

> What is truth? said jesting Pilate, and
> would not stay for an answer.
>
> Francis Bacon, "Of Truth"

The answer never seems to come on time.
But when it comes, it's just in time.

Note: "… even so come …" (Charlotte Brontë, *Jane Eyre*).

Please pardon our irresolution.

4262. Past "the province of literature"

Milton was steeped through and through with classical literature. ... They did not sweeten his naturally disagreeable temper. ... But in the province of literature where their influence is soonest and most powerfully exerted, they conferred on him all the benefits which the encomiasts ascribe to them. The dignity, the sanity ... which ennoble Virgil and the great Greeks ... are all to be found in Milton.

A. E. Housman, "Introductory Lecture," delivered before the Faculties of Arts and Laws and of Science, University College, London, October 3, 1892

You can call it hubris, or you can call it something happier: some of us who know a lot less classical literature than Milton are still hoping to get a little more out of the little we do know of it. Personally, I'm actually hoping that it will, a little, improve my disposition. After all that murder and anger and trying to get back home; all that loving and hating, on the battlefields and bedrooms and the places in-between; all that betrayal and all that trying to be loyal (even under the full weight of a father's body and the hunger to have the bodies of others), and then, sometimes, buckling at the knees, and falling: *all our woe* (Milton, *Paradise Lost*), all of it, and then some—something more—something better: something above and beyond anything that comes from all the parsing out of winning from losing; homecoming from wandering; founding from finishing; Falling from Rising; having, from having not. There's plenty to learn from those separations, of course. They're all there, in the Classic Style; all there, in black and white and black and blue all over. But maybe something more confusing (and thus clarifying) dwells amongst those bowers and battalions as well: maybe something else lurks above and below all those mortal differences, something strange and sweet, ready to teach us to forget, for a while, our differences; something ready to receive us (at least in some comparative language of compassion into which *we* might translate and receive *it*); some language of compassion, like what awaits a warrior come home to a place that knows him by his real name. Can anyone ever really acquire such a grammar of confusion? I hope so. *But* if so,

---

Note: "still more is demanded of us" (Ernst Robert Curtius, "The Personnel of the Comedia," *European Literature and the Latin Middle Ages*).

4267. "I'll come and see you again, as soon as I can"

> I may be gone for a good while; but I'll come
> and see you again, as soon as I can.
>
> J.R.R. Tolkien, *The Fellowship of the Ring*

Someone who's been helping you out and whom you expected to stay for a while (maybe forever) abruptly announces his immediate departure for parts unknown. Why he's going is bigger than the both of you—too big for him to say; too big for you to see. He says he'll be back, but he doesn't say when.

That sucks.

But then you remember something that makes his sudden leaving a little easier. He's been a help to you because he keeps his word to you. So you figure, if says he'll be back, he'll be back.

And then you go about your business. You've done the best you can to trust one for the team.

Note: "Being is the most intelligible and at the same time concealment" (Heidegger, *Basic Concepts*).

4269. "He ... gave me clues to keep me afloat in the conversational stream"

> From the moment we fell in love he knew instinctively how to help me cover my blank spots. ... He had a clear, resonant voice. He never seemed to raise it, and I always heard what he said; at least he let me think I did. When we were with other people he watched to see how I was doing and when I floundered he unobtrusively gave me clues to keep me afloat in the conversational stream.
>
> qtd. by Erving Goffman, from *Stigma: Notes on the Management of Spoiled Identity*

I hope this doesn't sound like some ancient history: a husband helping his wife seem like she's swimming along in conversations, even though it's hard for her to hear them (she'd have sunk otherwise).

He's gone now.

Maybe she's learned to look like she's keeping up with the flow, without him. Or maybe she's found friends (lifeguards and swim instructors of various kinds) who have taught her the strokes she needs to mark her own way across even the coldest channels.

Yesterday's "wide water, without sound" (Wallace Stevens, "Sunday Morning") could turn on to today's current of connectivity.

All it needs is a little lining.

Note: "Whispers antiphonal in azure swing" (Hart Crane, "Atlantis," *The Bridge*)

4270. "poor Marcus Aurelius"

> Poor Marcus Aurelius is obliged to write pages and pages in order to be able to find the inner disposition that he should normally have.
>
> Pierre Hadot, "Philosophy as Life and as a Quest for Wisdom"

All I can say is I know how he feels. There's this great Closer-Scene in a movie called *Say Anything*, with John Cusack on a plane with his girlfriend, coaxing her to calmness as they're taking off (she's afraid of flying—she's afraid of most things). So there he is sitting next to her, talking softly to her, telling her that once the light indicating that passengers are free to unbuckle goes on, it'll all be good. He keeps repeating this to her (with variations), as the wings go up, and we reach our cruising altitude; he keeps talking and talking until the light goes on and, in the same flash and click, the movie ends.

So here we are sitting on this weirdly dimensioned Plane together. We're a little scared. (We're a little scared of most things.) And maybe we're talking too much (we're talking a lot, that's for sure), waiting to lift off or fall asleep. Then maybe someone else sitting near enough to us to say something, says something (it could be anything), and it's just enough flash and click, no matter the vision and volume of the Tumult that sets and besets us, to release us. *Then there we are!* (Henry James, *The Ambassadors*)—*Both parties …*

Note:

swore to terms of peace
set by their arbiter, Athena, daughter
of Zeus who bears the stormcloud as a shield—
Though she still kept the form and voice of Mentor.
(*The Odyssey* last lines, trans. Robert Fitzgerald)

DECEMBER 2012

4275. “her endless power of surrender”

She balanced, intensely, for the lingering moment, almost with a terror of her endless power of surrender.

Henry James, *The Golden Bowl*

Have you ever noticed how *surrender* and *surround* sort of sound the same? (It’s kind of like how *Dog* is *God* spelled backward.) Coincidence? I think so—but maybe it’s more than that, too. Given how much must take itself from us, we have to hope that what leaves us all the time will stop to linger, from time to time (if only to regain its balance after tripping on some terror), in the infinite light of all our embracing love.

Note: The “sacrament of execution” (James, *The Golden Bowl*) “which ... he made his own” (Laurence B. Holland, “The Redemptive Process,” *The Expense of Vision: Essays on the Craft of Henry James*).

4281. “Not a creature was stirring”

’Twas the night before Christmas, when all through the house
Not a creature was stirring, not even a ...

Clement Clarke Moore, “A Visit from St. Nicholas”

Remember your first time with your first rhyme? The voice of a parent pausing before you, so that you could sound out the last part yourself? It's evident: we're always a little returned to the sound of our childhood—caught up in some music, made before the Age of Reason—when our ears will hear nothing but the soundness of rhyme. "'Rime,' says Henry Lanz, 'is one of those irrational satellites that revolve around reason'" (W. K. Wimsatt, "One Relation of Rhyme to Reason"). The lines between the rhymes may get out there, all right—like flying reindeer carrying some old man who gives us all he's got—but they'll come back to planet earth in good time. Remember how the space between its beginning and its end was (still is) the opposite of scary? It's not like the silence that lasts forever—*The eternal silence of these infinite spaces*, the eternal silence that *frightens me* (Pascal).

It's more like the silence you know will always give way to a click of two heels that calls you back home.

Note: "mouse" (see above).

4284. The Portal's Tale

> The doorway is an opening made in a wall to permit entrance and exit from one area to another. If it is monumental or embellished with decorations, the doorway becomes a portal.
>
> Francesca Prina, *Architecture: Elements, Materials, Form*

I don't remember exactly when I came to feel a portal. It seems only last night that I was just another pilgrim passing through. But over the course of time, so many fellow travelers stopped me on the way to hear the stories I could tell them, and to tell, in turn, the stories they could tell me, that after a thousand and one nights detained by these tales, I finally fell asleep. Traveling in my dreams through gates of horn and ivory, I woke to find that I had become more passageway than passenger.

No one would wonder at the wound of vacancy that must occupy, now and then, the position of portal. *(Are you leaving already? It seems like you just got here.)* But all these *so many partings*, even the most painful, are *welded together* (Dickens, *Great Expectations*), and on balance, I like being this way, and would not wonder if I were not the only being who felt fit and full and fine, being this way.

Such is my story, and peace be on us all! ("The Porter and the Three Ladies of Baghdad," *The Arabian Nights*, trans. Sir Richard Burton).

Note

And what if all of animated nature
Be but organic Harps diversely framed,
That tremble into thought, as o'er them sweeps
Plastic and vast, one intellectual breeze,
At once the Soul of each, and God of all?
(Samuel Taylor Coleridge, "The Eolian Harp")

4291. The Life of Love

> Death is perhaps rediscovered in the unconscious as the most radical—but also most sterile—principle of its logic. But it is life which crystallizes the first objects to which desire attaches itself, before even thought can cling to them.
>
> Jean Laplanche, *Life and Death in Psychoanalysis*

So what we first love; what we love before we know it, gains its form and its luster—

> Whatever is fickle, freckled (who knows how?)
> With swift, slow; sweet, sour; adazzle dim
> (Hopkins, "Pied Beauty")

—from the force of life and not the fascinations of death? Is that right? I think so. And when our love becomes a conscious passion, it can keep some continuous faith with this aboriginal attachment to the Forms of Life that will surpass the Fascinations of Death? Is that right? I think so.

That is my understanding of the dark passage from the illuminated text that I have before me, and the Dark Passage illuminated outside my window that passes through me, and beyond me.

So, that's the story of my understanding, and for reasons I do not understand, I'm sticking to it. For reasons I will never understand, it has certainly stood by me.

Note: "Your remarks … summon up Eliot's 'These fragments I have shor'd up against my ruin.' … But I think it better not to make the allusion yourself but to allow the reader to make it on his own" (Mary McCarthy to Hannah Arendt, September 19, 1967).

4293. "a proficiency in telephoning and telegraphing"

I ha[ve] acquired a proficiency in telephoning and telegraphing which seems to have done away with my ability to express myself in less lapidary style.

Edith Wharton, letter to Corinne Roosevelt Robinson, March 2, 1914

Has the sheared volume of our talking and texting made us forget that any given signaling may be our last say (the chattering gleaming of our particular moment covertly engraving its permanent monument)? What with all those dropped calls and lost messages, you'd think we'd remember by now.

Maybe we remember, after all. Maybe that's why it's so hard to know how to stop. Maybe that's why we silently know how important it is when we do.

Note: "God knows whether we ever meet again!" (Austen, *Persuasion*).

4301. "an extraordinary mildness"

> Towards the end he sailed into an extraordinary
> mildness,
>
> Auden, "Herman Melville" (for Lincoln Kirstein)

I've never met a mildness that didn't seem extraordinary, and something toward the end: the smoothing something of a final act of forgiveness after a long, jagged drama of anger and anguish and being out at sea: some compassionate writing (*don't worry: it's all right*) that coaxes something upset to right its balance long enough to make its way back to port; some signal sent straight to a wayward heart that it's safe to come home; some memory of wholeness that recalls the amputated adventurer to the going grace of the last dance, just this side of the closing curtain.

Lately, I've been meeting with another mildness as well, twin of the first, I think, and no less extraordinary. It stretches toward a new start rather than the last rest—the one that comes after the big fall, but well before the final flight.

Note: "so tender and mild" ("Silent Night").

4304. "Mine would, sir, were I human"

Ariel: ... if you now beheld them, your affections
Would become tender.

Prospero: Dost thou think so, spirit?

Ariel: Mine would, sir, were I human.

Shakespeare, *The Tempest*

Not being a human being himself, the spirit settles instead for making someone who is a better one. He's like a poem or a page or a play or a pool that prepares its pupil to navigate the sea of tears that surrounds us. He's like the first song you heard about someone breaking up—the one you go back to whenever you're breaking up, yourself, to learn again some basic lessons in tenderness and decency under duress. He's like the strokes you were taught in your first swim lessons when, later, you suddenly find yourself really over your head and very far from shore. That's what he's like, and all you have to do is to remember what those like him have to teach you, and then, no matter how dark and stormy, you'll always make it back to where you have to be.

Note: "lessons at love's pain and heartache school" (Jackson Browne, "Fountain of Sorrow").

4306. "Make it up as we go along" (Talking Heads)

He always regarded himself as a failure: he
had not done what he once meant to do.

George Eliot, *Middlemarch*

Actually, I've gotten so busy doing what I'm doing that I don't really remember what I once meant to do.

I'm okay with that.

It's like what happens when, one way or another, we get all in with one another: who really remembers how we got started, or how we were supposed to end?

That *is success in life* (Pater): I mean, once we're really all here, who would want to be anywhere else?

Note: *in medias res.*

JANUARY 2013

4319. "whom I hopelessly love" 163

> he looks like my best friend my constant lover
> hopelessly loyal tawny and apt and whom I hopelessly love
>
> Frank O'Hara, "Cantata"

First he's talking about his cat and then his best friend, and then both. That's the great thing about praising. Once it really starts, there's really no stopping it.

Note: *disposto a salire a le stelle*—"ready to rise to the stars" (Dante, *Purgatorio*, Canto XXXIII, trans. Charles S. Singleton).

4324. Midlife Morning

> They had received their unlooked-for happiness as a free gift from their Creator's hands, and they submitted to its loss, not without sorrow, but without impious and stubborn repining.
>
> Hazlitt, "On Shakespeare and Milton"

Sometimes it's as easy as falling asleep after the longest day. Other times, it's as hard as waking up after some endless fight. And then, every once in a while, it's one of those mornings where you get up and, though you're not really sure why, you're just ready: *you're good to go.*

Note: "Through Eden took their solitary way" (Milton, *Paradise Lost*).

4327. "my dreams are not calm"

> One memorial of my former condition nevertheless remains: my dreams are not calm; the dread swell and agitation of the storm have not wholly subsided; the legions that encamped in them are drawing off, but not departed.
>
> De Quincey, *Confessions of an English Opium Eater*

Neither have mine, and I hope they never do. (It's lonely enough around here, as it is.) Those dream-remainders: they're like houseguests or expectant glances: I always worry I won't be up for them when they come, but, really, where would I be without them?

And where would we go, but with them?

Note: "My sleep is still tumultuous … like … Paradise to our first parents, when looking back from afar" (De Quincey).

FEBRUARY 2013

4339. Finding My *Picture of Dorian Gray* 165

You'd think I'd know exactly where it is, considering how much my life has depended on it. I mean how *much* of my life has depended on the Proud (I'm not proud of this pride, though sometimes I make believe that I am) conviction that I can keep it in its place, and present it where and how I see fit to present it—or feel it is fit to be presented. But the books that we teach and the faces that we feature are (come the final take) no more under our control than the kindness of our kids and the passing of our parents. I should know that by now, but I have to learn it all over again, all the time—just like I have to spend half my half-waking hours looking for a copy of that goddamn *Dorian Gray*. What the Hell is wrong with me? It's not like I haven't been here long enough—I should know where to find every single book I have, in every single place I live. Have I gotten hold of too many books, or am I just losing my grip? Either way, it's just one more sign of getting old—of relinquishing what I really never had in the first place.

Now where *is* that book? It's not like I don't have hundreds of copies. And right now, I'd even settle for one of those half-assed prurient, "popular," paperback editions of it, published back in the day when I was born.

This is ridiculous. If people had any idea how much time I sacrifice searching for things I've already read, they'd lock me up in the attic, along with the crazy first wife and the embarrassing pictures.

Oh wait. Here it is.

Maybe I wouldn't have to spend so much time looking for it, if I took just a little trouble to make it feel at home—

Note: "recognized who it was" (Oscar Wilde, *The Picture of Dorian Gray*).

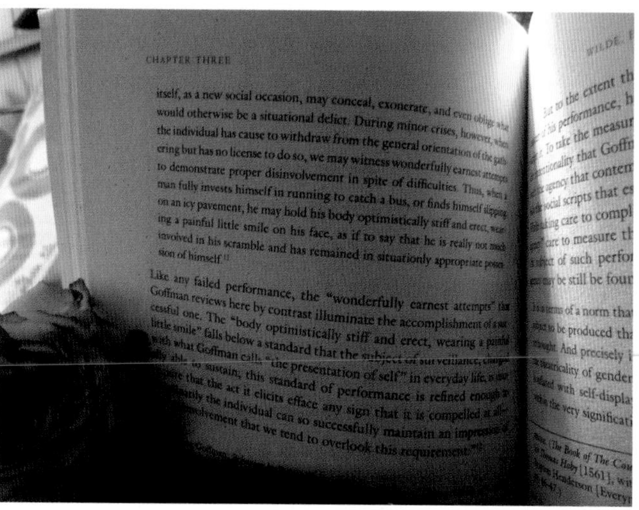

CHAPTER THREE

itself, as a new social occasion, may conceal, exonerate, and even oblige what
would otherwise be a situational delict. During minor crises, however, when
the individual has cause to withdraw from the general orientation of the gath-
ering but has no license to do so, we may witness wonderfully earnest attempts
to demonstrate proper disinvolvement in spite of difficulties. Thus, when a
man fully invests himself in running to catch a bus, or finds himself slipping
on an icy pavement, he may hold his body optimistically stiff and erect, wear-
ing a painful little smile on his face, as if to say that he is really not much
involved in his scramble and has remained in situationly appropriate posses-
sion of himself.[11]

Like any failed performance, the "wonderfully earnest attempts" that
Goffman reviews here by contrast illuminate the accomplishment of a suc-
cessful one. The "body optimistically stiff and erect, wearing a painful
little smile" falls below a standard that the subject of surveillance, charged
with what Goffman calls "the presentation of self" in everyday life, is
... able to sustain, this standard of performance is refined enough to
... that the act it elicits efface any sign that it is compelled at all
... the individual can so successfully maintain an impression of
... involvement that we tend to overlook this requirement."

"The author regrets the grammatical blemish" (Jeff Nunokawa, "Oscar Wilde, Erving Goffman and the Social Body Beautiful").

4349. "I have heard the mermaids singing, each to each"

T. S. Eliot, "The Love Song of J. Alfred Prufrock"

—oh, I've heard a lot of amazing creatures sing and say a lot of amazing things. And I still do—every day of the week, and sometimes twice on Sundays. I want to tell you the secret of my continuing hearing, because someday (maybe not today, but maybe someday, ten years or fifty years from today), it may come in handy for you: I don't worry, like I used to worry, whether what I'm hearing is meant for my ears. Now, when I listen to people talk about what or who or how they love, I don't care as much as I once did, if they're talking about me, or even to me. I'm just glad that the waves of sound are so pitched with devotion.

If this sounds too good to be true, all I can say is that it seems like all the truest goods sound too good to be true—something as good as clearing (slow or swift) from deafness to delight, or a change in the mood of a verb, or a vision, that gives a new form of life to the most tried and tired drab directions.

"You can't hear God speak to someone else, you can hear him only if you are being addressed."—That is a grammatical remark (Wittgenstein). But grammar can be transformed at the speed of a dream or the shift of a continent, and before you know it, you could wind up at a case where you can *only* hear what you might call God speaking to someone else; *never* when you are being addressed, alone.

In any case, that's all I have to say to you. And I'll leave you in peace now, since I know you have plenty to talk about amongst yourselves.

Note: "poetry is *over*heard" (John Stuart Mill, "What Is Poetry?").

BILINGUAL EDITION
EDITED BY G.E.M. Anscombe and G.H. von Wrig

4350. "I was part of the nastiness now"

Raymond Chandler, *The Big Sleep*

Being around kids learning that for the first time makes me remember how quickly I forget that I've been a part of it for a long time.

Great Awakenings: you never know when they start. And you never know where they'll end. Some of the sweetest risings I've ever seen began on a street that can be mighty mean.

Note: "I would pray that we learn to treat one another with mutual civilities" (Cotton Mather, "Of Poetry and Style").

4351. When What You Say Comes Out Just Right

There are moments when speech is but a mouth pressed
Lightly and humbly against the angel's hand.

James Merrill, "A Dedication"

A friend calls: his heart is in trouble. You don't know how much trouble. Neither does he. You talk to him for a while and then you hang up and you think: "that wasn't right." So you call him back. And this time when you hang up, you know that he feels a little better. You don't remember a thing that you said to him (the memory, already muffled).

And you know that it really doesn't matter.

Note: "How could we define this more specifically than by love?" (Kierkegaard, *Philosophical Fragments*).

4352. From Wary to Wonder

C'est une grande habileté que de savoir cacher son habileté
(It is a great cleverness to know how to hide one's cleverness.)

La Rochefoucauld

And then there's what's hidden beyond all the end-zones; some new field where feeling clever falls into something softer: where hard-ass offensive and defensive positions (the fake-out, first of all) have faded out—like your last mean, merely domestic, thought, before a foreign movie resolved enough to really startle you out of your customary senses. And then there you are, moving along (more like streaming than stepping on); there you are, and your feelings are slowly motioning from clever to curious: like you're suddenly in a new city in another decade and another country, and you come upon these strange structures, and you can't figure out how anyone could make them. At first, you don't even know what to make of them—beyond amazement.

And then you remember: Philosophy doesn't start with a win. Philosophy begins in wonder.

Note

Oh do not ask, "What is it?"
Let us go and make our visit.
(T. S. Eliot, "The Love Song of J. Alfred Prufrock")

4355. "Having survived entirely your own youth"

James Merrill, "Discothèque"

—wait: did I survive it, or did it survive me? Either way, I'm glad *someone* survived. And I'm hoping that the one who did won't forget the one who didn't.

Note: "connected together by chains of affinities" (Darwin, *The Origin of Species*).

4359. "prevented him from burning the difficult beginnings"

> It was in an Ithaca backyard that his wife prevented him from burning the difficult beginnings of *Lolita*, which was completed in 1953.

John Updike, "An Introduction to Nabokov's Lectures"

Of course, some things are best left undone. Not everything you start turns into a great novel, or some other form of knowing about the terrible things that people do to one another. And even less turns up anything like a feasible plan to stop any of those terrible things.

Still though, you never know. "*Lolita* ... was completed in 1953." Now, when I think of 1953, I start thinking about 1954.

1954—Big Year: If you were on *Jeopardy* (personally, I prefer the original, with Art Fleming and Don Pardo—I'm Old School that way), and the category was "Landmark Supreme Court Decisions" and the clue was "1954," I'll bet you'd know the correct answer as well as you'd know to phrase it as a question: "What is *Brown versus Board of Education*?"

"What is *Brown v. Board of Education?*" you ask? Well, like that book by Nabokov, it's partly about students in distress. It's partly about saving them a little from the terrible things that people do to one another.

Trains of thought; Antecedent principles; Nervous laughter: It's funny how once things get started, you don't know how they'll end.

And you'll never know if you don't see them through.

Note: "problems ... still await a solution" (George Lichtheim, *Thoughts Among the Ruins*).

4360. Cold Gathering

> Here loveless birds now flock as winter friends.
>
> Robert Frost, "A Winter Eden"

Maybe you wonder when you first arrive: which came first, the friendship or the flocking? But after you've been at the party for a while, and feeling a lot less loveless, you're just glad to be among so many with whom you've come to feel at home.

Whichever the way that got you there, you're
content with bud inspecting. ("A Winter Eden")

Note: "We see the other not simply as an individual but ... as a cohabitant of the same specific world" (Simmel, "How Is Society Possible?").

MARCH 2013

4366. My Mother, and Welcome to Her!

> There can be no question that [the] death of Proust's mother coincided with a profound "crisis," but ... the writing of *In Search of Lost Time* started up only well after her death.
>
> Roland Barthes, "The Work as Will,"
> *The Preparation of the Novel*

I wonder if it could start up well before? Imagine preparing for your mother's death by means of a record of some lost time, with her as its sometimes secret center. Imagine trying to make that record a matter of public record, something ready to remind you of your interest in the world, even after the passing of the person who first made you feel at home there. Imagine drawing on her Old School sense of Good Citizenship in the hope that her consolidated memory will keep your own sense of it in good standing, no matter what private catastrophe might interrupt it. (Speaking of *Res Publica*, the other night, my mom cut our usual conversation short, because she didn't want to be even one percent late for the annual meeting of her condominium association. I discovered later that only nine righteous residents attended. I have yet to discover what, if anything, they discussed.)

Going on without our parents: it's like those pilgrims in covered wagons my mother always claims as ancestors, cattle ranchers who wound up settling a long way from where they started. *You're from Pioneer Stock, though you'd never know it!* she likes to say to me.

But the truth is that we both know that I do.

Note: *Et cuius erant nisi tua verba illa per matrem meam, fidelem tuam, quae cantasti in aures meas?* (S. Avgvstini, *Confessionvm*, "Liber II").

4367. "difficult marvels"

The child upon
The bank, hands full of difficult marvels

James Merrill, "The Black Swan"

Sometimes the difficulties that keep your hands full all day change into marvels that make your heart ache at night. It's like in a musical, when a quarreling couple, at the speed of sound, sing their way back to love.

That's how you know there's something like magic. That's when you feel you're somehow alive.

Note: "being a continued Allegory" (Edmund Spenser, "Prefatory Letter").

4372. "vanished early"

> but her bloom had vanished early
>
> Jane Austen, *Persuasion*

I've never seen a bloom that vanished *late*. As far as I can see, everything around that *could* vanish, vanished sooner than I would've guessed—blossomings, bruisings, etc.

Maybe we'll get to know each other better in a later life: our root causes, our random effects and our every variation in between. Who knows, maybe what's vanished from us will return for us in some different form, weathered and wiser and gentler now, and ready to take us back.

And then you can finally tell him that, as far as you could see, he'd never really gone away in the first place.

Note: "I have loved none but you" (*Persuasion*).

4378. "I have now at last become a writer only"

F. Scott Fitzgerald, "Handle with Care,"
part 3 of *The Crack-Up*

At least I have at night—but that's a big *at least:* maybe not a least as Big as the Ritz—but still, it's something major (even if only from the mine of one mind).

Still, it's something seriously new—an avenue found for an avenue lost: all the other driving that *must* be done by dawn has taken its engines elsewhere. (I know which Streets.)

That just leaves me writing.

Who?

The who without ignitions, trying to write to you.

Note: "still stream" (Keats, "Ode to a Nightingale").

4383. Something Given from Somewhere Hidden

gather thee,—
Cresses that grow where no man may them see

Keats, "Endymion: A Poetic Romance"

I'll bet you want to bring someone something like that. And you probably think that first you have to figure out where to find it.

But maybe it's the other way around. Maybe first you really have to love someone enough to want to give her something hidden; love her enough to want to give her something still growing, from way-back-when, before you stand any real chance of ever really getting to that place where you find the thing you really want her to really have.

Note: "wild surmise" (Keats, "On First Looking into Chapman's Homer").

4384. "busy seeking for otters"

> Coll and his dogs and Joseph were busy seeking
> for otters, of which this island has many.
>
> James Boswell, *Journal of a Tour to the Hebrides*

I love an island with many otters. At least I love it now. I love Coll and his dogs and Joseph. At least I love them now. I love people busy seeking while I am sleeping, or seeking elsewhere.

I love the golden intention, the pure soul of seeking for something that only the seeker can see. I love to remember my father with his friend, fishing for hours from a small boat on the bay in front of our house. (Did they ever catch anything?) I love to recall the exultation rising from a basement in Nyack, New York—the sound of two men succeeding in fixing something that meant nothing to anyone else.

Some kind of victory, someone upstairs murmured.

None sweeter, I said to myself at the time.

Note: "They are the Yea or Nay of that good for which men are enduring and fighting. In these delicate vessels is borne onward through the ages the treasure of human affections" (George Eliot, *Daniel Deronda*).

4386. "this penetrative suggestion of life"

It is in this penetrative suggestion of life.

Walter Pater, "The Poetry of Michelangelo"

You always worry about the wreckage that results from any kind of break-in, no matter how discreet the intruder—until you remember the other side of the same odd story: what damages, defines.

I mean, when was the last time you heard of a China Shop that didn't have a Bull in it?

Note: "This charmed and temperate space" (Pater, "Michelangelo").

4388. Making Up in the Middle of the Night

An actress ... had been studying a part and
rehearsing it ... suddenly, on the stage ... beg[an]
to improvise, to speak lines not in the text.

Henry James, *The Golden Bowl*
(tense of the original modified)

The only salvation from darkness (or its daytime derivative, dullness) I've ever really known comes when someone says something to me that I wasn't expecting her to say—something crazy or considerate enough to loosen and lighten up all the usual cordial and cool shows that draw us apart as much as they draw us together.

It's the only time I ever really feel forgiven; the only time I ever really feel ready to start fresh.

He did something wrong somewhere along the line, my mother explained to me tonight, when I asked her to summarize why Moses, according to the story, wasn't allowed to enter the Promised Land, after all those years wandering around in the desert.

Here's the good news: turns out there's always more than one line.

Note: "It should be possible to breach … expectancies … surprise is possible" (Harold Garfinkel, *Studies in Ethnomethodology*).

4390. "The scars were of different ages"

> I saw three well-known trees; in front, the bark was worn smooth, as if by the breast of … [a jaguar], and on each side, there were deep scratches, or rather grooves, extending in an oblique line. … The scars were of different ages.
>
> Charles Darwin, "Buenos Ayres and St. Fe," *The Voyage of the Beagle*

There are good reasons for believing that Charles Darwin had a finer eye for the gradations of age than I do. I'm looking at one right here. See, in my book, all scars are more or less the same age: as soon as a scratch (or some deeper cut) becomes a scar, it all at once becomes no younger or older than any other scar. Once a wound has made a permanent mark, the particular date and duration of its actual birth and being fade into a common era, and put on the same uniform—like the free-agent pang that the team of pain can always recruit, as one of its own, for any given scrimmage.

And then, of course, there are all the smooth areas between the scars. *Your hands are so smooth*, a soccer player said to me this morning at breakfast. Then I showed her my callouses and then, naturally, she showed me the scars on her legs.

Those must have hurt, I said.

I don't remember how she answered. There were too many girls saying too many species of quick, bright things to keep the lines of descent unconfused. The whole sunburst sequence blurred together in the fast, fixing, first light that starts the promise of any old, new day.

Note: "Monuments of unaging" (Yeats, "Sailing to Byzantium").

APRIL 2013

4399. "I have promises to keep" 181

Robert Frost, "Stopping by Woods on a Snowy Evening"

And you try your best to keep them. Maybe even the ones you can't remember making. Maybe even those the most.

Note: "Haunted for ever by the eternal mind" (Wordsworth, "Intimations" Ode).

4400. Self-Doubt for Adults

his inward objector

George Eliot, *Daniel Deronda*

I just heard from mine. It's been a while, and I'm glad to be in touch—especially since I see how he's changed.

He used to come bearing threats that people would turn their back on me.

Now he's come to ask me not to turn my back on *them*.

4401. "for the party"

She owned that, considering every thing, she was not absolutely without inclination for the party.

Jane Austen, *Emma*

There's always some moving part within you that wants to take part in some party beyond.

Some nights (some scarred and scared nights), that's the only flicker of light you feel.

Some nights (some sweet and starry nights), that's the only proof of life you need.

Note: "past the circuit of the lamp's thin flame" (Hart Crane, *The Bridge*).

4402. "compelled her to grace"

"You love me very, very much, Izz?" he suddenly asked.
"I do. …"

"More than Tess?"

She shook her head. "No," she murmured: "not more than she."

"How's that?"

"Because nobody could love 'ee more than Tess did! … She would have laid down her life for 'ee. I could do no more." …

[T]he fascination exercised over her rougher nature by Tess's character compelled her to grace.

Thomas Hardy, *Tess of the D'Urbervilles*

The girl can't help herself. An awe as strong as any oath obliges her to tell the truth, even though telling it costs her everything she wants.

It's a little like the love that provokes the girl's awe in the first place: ready to give all.

Some of the best love going feels like that: like an imitation of love that never hopes to rise to the level of the love that it admires.

I mean, doesn't what we call love sometimes come down to putting the interests of others above our own?

Note: "In boy; go first" (Shakespeare, *King Lear*).

4403. "impulses which she had not known before"

Rosamund had delivered her soul under impulses
which she had not known before.

George Eliot, *Middlemarch*

It always feels like the first time: the spirit that moves us to reach one another.

And it always feels like it doesn't matter if it's the last.

Note: "Magically escaped" (Walter Benjamin, "The Storyteller").

4404. "There are as many perfections as there are imperfect men"

Wilde, "The Soul of Man Under Socialism"

One more, actually: the perfection of the power to tell them apart and then put them back together again.

Note: "Let me count the ways" (Elizabeth Barrett Browning, *Sonnets from the Portuguese*, "XLIII").

4405. Reserve Army of Rescuers

You know the type—always *true to his ancient habit of happening to be everywhere where he had no business* (Dickens, *Great Expectations*). He's always somewhere he doesn't belong—except when he's not: like when he's rescuing the man whose ancient habit is to think him always somewhere he doesn't belong.

Next time, the soul the suddenly salient loiterer saves may well be your own.

Note: "spare vivacity" (*Great Expectations*).

4406. The Charmed Cycle

> The … philosophy of disillusion … he thinks all that a prejudice.
>
> Walter Pater, "Sir Thomas Browne"

Sometimes, when you're tired, all your enthusiasms feel like so many found-out fallacies, so many *detected illusions* (George Eliot), so many lost loves. But they're never really lost. They're more like idols gone idle in the twilight, ready at a morning's notice to turn over and turn into better reasons for loving and believing than the ones you lost the night before.

Love that.

Note:

> When half-gods go,
> The gods arrive.
> (Emerson, "Give All to Love")

4407. "Only he and his opponent … knew that he was being destroyed"

G.L.S.

It reminds one of all those equal and opposite situations where only two people know that one of them has kept the other from destruction: the one who did the saving and the one who did the getting saved.

Note: "Never forget what you have done …" (George Eliot, *Middlemarch*).

4408. Self-Reliance for Commoners

> The nonchalance of boys who are sure of a dinner, and would disdain as much as a lord to do or say aught to conciliate one, is the healthy attitude of human nature.
>
> Emerson, "Self Reliance"

I don't know anyone *that* self-confident (though I've seen a lot of people, myself included, act as if they were). The people I know, myself included, have to settle in with the next best strength: the power to live with the pang of knowing that there isn't enough approval in all the world to ease the ache that wants it.

Note: "my true fate" (John Ashbery, "A Boy").

4415. What to Love

> Love only what … is destined for you.
>
> Marcus Aurelius, *Meditations*

But how do you know what you're destined to love, until you start to love it?

Note: "there's both my hands, Miss" (Dickens, *Our Mutual Friend*).

4418. "funny"

> How funny you are today New York
> like Ginger Rogers in *Swingtime.*
>
> Frank O'Hara, "Steps"

Like a quirky city or a crazy stretch, she doesn't think she's strange. That's why she seems so funny. That's how you fall in love.

JUNE 2013

4405. "an endlesse moniment"

for short time an endlesse moniment

Edmund Spenser, "Epithalamion"

Sometimes I get discouraged when I realize that most of what I write will never see much light of day. But then I remember how some of the best practices aren't aimed to reach past the ages, but rather just to get us through the night.

Note: "All he wanted to do was get him and his sister safely home" (Harper Lee, *To Kill a Mockingbird*).

4409. "for poetry was all written before time was"

Emerson, "The Poet"

I think that's why it can be such a good friend when you're unhappy, and every cause you can come up with for being so seems like so many settings after some lost fact, before all the clocks (some Temple destroyed, some Terror unleashed).

As long as you don't get hung up on too many questions about who, when, where, and why, the best poems will open a dedicated line to some place past all the time zones, a dedicated line, just for you.

Then all you have to do is be a little open, too.

Note: "surrounding ourselves with the original circumstances" (Emerson, "History").

4410. "What they made of his lectures is not known"

In addition to the more usual subjects, he taught the schoolboys philosophy. What they made of his lectures is not known.

Peter Singer on Hegel's years as a high school teacher, in *Hegel: A Very Short Introduction*

I wonder if any of those boys made of the lectures given to them by that prominent purveyor of dialectical thought anything like what a girl made of my lectures on American literature at the posh high school in a posh part of Los Angeles where I briefly taught many years ago.

The girl was poor and didn't live anywhere near the school. I sometimes wondered how she got there.

She must have caught the bus.

What she was learning from our class she told me one day was that people both in literature and in life strengthened the sense of who they were by discovering who they were not. She was grateful to the school where we met. She understood that the scholarship it gave her to go there was her ticket to a better life, both for herself personally and, by extension, for the people she loved.

But she was grateful for another reason as well. By showing her who she wasn't, the school was also showing her who she was.

I used to worry a bit about her. She was doing well enough in the class, but she seemed a little lonely.

After that conversation, though, I never worried about her again.

Note: "the suffering … and the labor of the negative" (Hegel).

4411. "And in short, I was afraid"

T. S. Eliot, "The Love Song of J. Alfred Prufrock"

Sometimes the "long story short" version is the only one you can bear to tell. Other times, it's the only one you can't.

Note: "it is not easy to foresee a natural end" (Freud, "Analysis Terminable and Interminable").

4413. "the pleasure of giving respect"

He did not remember the pleasure of giving respect.

Tobias Wolff, "Bullet in the Brain"

—which can only mean that he didn't remember the pleasure of receiving it, either.

Oh, and how about those times—the best times of all—when giving and receiving respect are so welded together that there's really no telling them apart?

Note: "There remains yet something of honor and pride, of life" (William Faulkner, *Light in August*).

JULY 2013

4415. Of Bragging

According to a friend, Lord Byron loved to brag, even about his accomplishments in areas of endeavor where his clubbed foot would have prevented him from going very far:

> He bragged, too, of his prowess in riding, boxing, fencing, and even walking: but to excel in these things feet are as necessary as hands. (*His Very Self and Voice: Collected Conversations of Lord Byron*, ed. Ernest J. Lovell Jr.)

Speaking of what's necessary, I guess we're all wounded and wanting enough to need to brag at least little, just to make our stand, and stumble our way through life. Of course, no one wants to be thought of as a bragger—just as no one wants to be thought quite unable to score the goals that he brags about.

That would be as hard as abandoning all hope that we might ever do the things we have so far only dreamed of doing.

Note: "He's still a little bitch!" (a Young Friend on Cristiano Ronaldo).

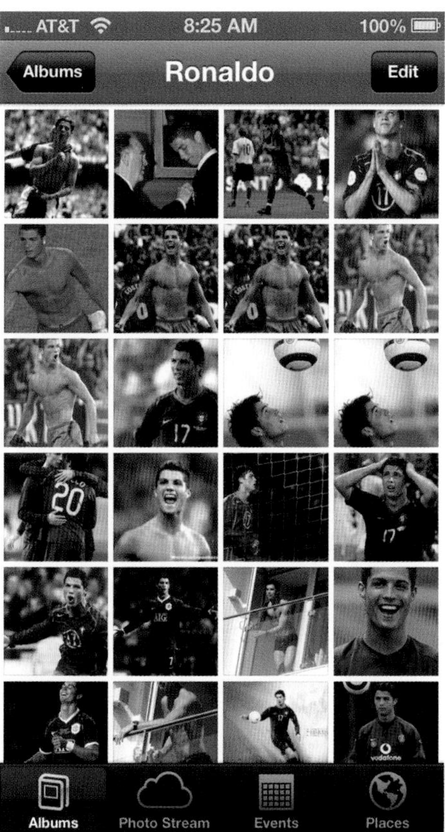

4417. "writing at tension's limit"

> writing at tension's limit [escritura en el límite de la tensión]
>
> Roberto Bolaño, "There Are No Rules" [No Hay Reglas]

It's like driving at night on the edges of a foreign town or a foreign time where you wish you knew the language, but you don't. You wish you knew the language, because you're scared of what's strange and also because you half-remember knowing it once and half-believe that if you could only knew it again, the fear that makes it so hard for you to love would disappear like a tense and fallacious border, exposed to the light of day.

Meanwhile, you keep your eye on the lines. Pretty soon the sun will come up, and it'll be time for you to stop and rest.

Note: "When the light that's lost within us reaches the sky" (Jackson Browne, "Before the Deluge").

4419. "almost converted"

almost converted by [her] ardour

George Eliot, *Middlemarch*

Maybe the best ardours only *almost* convert. Maybe their best authors know that "only" by heart.

Note: "Her finely touched spirit had still its fine issues" (*Middlemarch*).

4420. "as if I, not they, were leaving"

Addio, one or two will say, leb' wohl,
And press my hand as if I, not they, were leaving.
Look for us. We have chosen—no—you chose.

James Merrill, "The Opera Company"

Weeks and months go by where you feel a little lonelier with each passing Act. Is it some higher altitude, or some lowering one, that seems to thin out the atmosphere of love? Have they left you, or you left them? When did you stop believing you could know the difference? How did the Grand Life of show-and-tell and promise come to feel like someone else's Big Reveal, spoken and sung in some romantic language, now nowhere near your own?

And you know that this feeling forlorn is partly just the season: the Season of Losses. You're pretty sure you'll get some of your old Play back. Maybe even some of the same stars (the ones you've not completely failed, the ones not faded from you, forever) will return to play their old roles—or maybe the parts of their parents. (It wouldn't be the first time.)

Meanwhile, though, you pay your respects as best you can to what you've lost and what you've left. Whatever the cost of its admission, compared to its cost of departure, it was basically free of charge.

Note: "The point will be to close with their exact words" ("The Opera Company").

4424. "up again old heart!"

> Never mind the ridicule, never mind the defeat: up again old heart! ... there is victory yet for all justice; and the true romance which the world exists to realize.
>
> Emerson, "Experience"

Well, there's no "never minding" it.

Sometimes (lots of times) you feel like a total fool, trying to imagine that things are better than they are, and thus helping to make them worse.

Sometimes (lots of times) ever louder, ever nearer, paid promulgators seem to ever more threaten to drown out your unsponsored sentiments. (How can they compete? It's like a rowboat showing up to show up an Armada.)

Sometimes (lots of times) the Defeat feels so bad and blanketing (like a sickness that could keep you in bed forever) that standing up seems like more than you can stand.

But you get up anyway. There's that *true* romance which the world you love *exists to realize*. There's that victory yet for *all* justice. There's that memory of your mother getting you to rise and shine, when it was still dark out, to face the day. There's that promise you made to keep it together and keep on moving as close as you can get to some Promised Land you'll never get to yourself. There's that quickening sense that comes from some phrase where the forces of compassion, conviction, and command converge.

There's that. There's more. You look. You listen. Then you make your move.

Up.

Note: "up again old heart!" (Emerson, "Experience").

4427. "irrevocably a poet"

> He became, as he relates, irrevocably a poet.
>
> Samuel Johnson, "Life of Cowley," *Lives of the English Poets*

All those things you've said that you wish you could take back and know you never can: all those words that disconnected a conversation or destroyed a friendship or determined a divorce: all those words that brought on bitterness and blighted brightness: words that ruined the joy of love, leaving it awkward or anguished: all those words that were one or two—or two hundred—too many, or one or two—or two hundred—too few: all the indelible damage—*all our woe* (Milton)—done by those irrevocable words: you think they might just have been enough to make you forever hold your peace.

Listen, though. Listen: Can you hear yourself now?—turns out they were just enough to make you care more than you ever thought you could, about what you say, and how you say it.

Note:

> With the farming of a verse
> Make a vineyard of the curse.
> (Auden for Yeats)

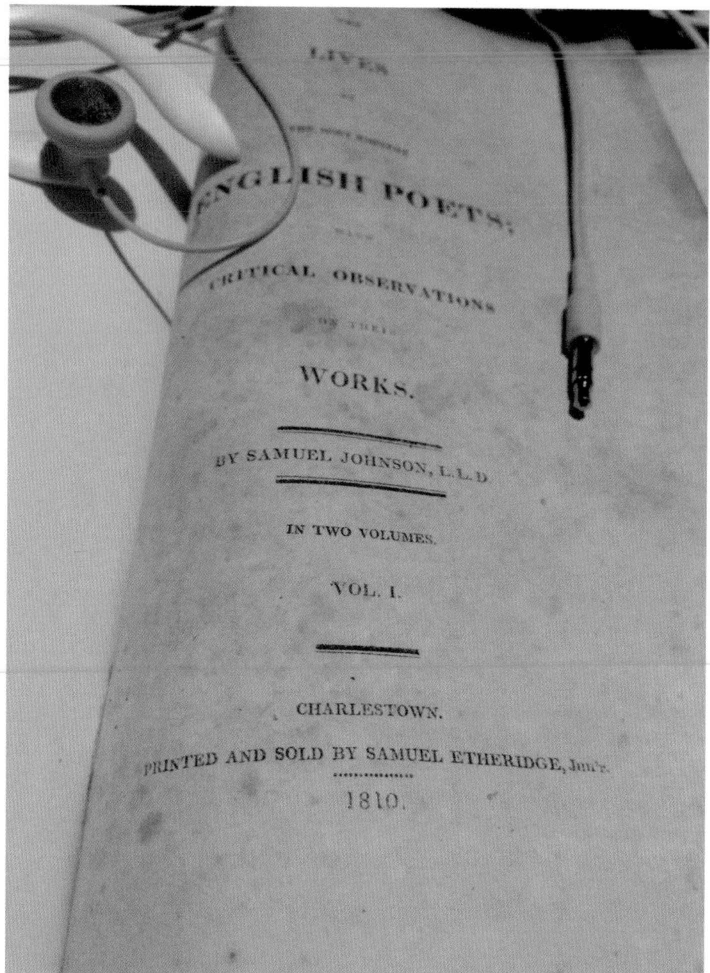

LIVES

ENGLISH POETS;

CRITICAL OBSERVATIONS

WORKS.

BY SAMUEL JOHNSON, L.L.D

IN TWO VOLUMES.

VOL. I.

CHARLESTOWN.

PRINTED AND SOLD BY SAMUEL ETHERIDGE, Jun'r.

1810.

4430. "speechless wonder"

> The inexpressible which, in seeking expression, will ultimately burst the too fragile vessel of earthly form by the infinite power of its being … the clarity of vision is immediately destroyed, and all that remains is speechless wonder.
>
> F. Creuzer, qtd. by Walter Benjamin in *The Origin of German Tragic Drama*

That's a little melodramatic for my taste. I'm more taken up by how close we earthly types, with all our showing and telling, can come to the limit of our powers of expression, and pull back before we fall off the stage and break our legs. There, we are, at the edge of what we can say ("The rest is silence." *Hamlet*), our parts, props, and propositions stirred and shaken, but not shattered.

Here we are, at our words' end, quiet and amazed at how much we have been led to describe the Deep of the Dark, without falling into it forever.

Note:

We are such stuff
As dreams are made on.
(*The Tempest*)

4432. "not mentioned because it is the whole of the story"

> a pathos not mentioned because it is the whole of the story
>
> William Empson, "Milton and Bentley,"
> *Some Versions of the Pastoral*

More and more you come to know the sadness at the story's center you never come to know.

Note: "Instead we made do with lifelong friendship" (James Merrill, *A Different Person: A Memoir*).

4433. "our togetherness"

Guard our togetherness from ghostly ills.

Auden, "The Age of Anxiety"

Actually, the way I see it, our togetherness may be the only thing that *doesn't* require protection from ghostly ills—the anguish of the ancestors that flares up now and then and threatens to ruin everything, like so many Biblical Plagues or Dysfunctional Relationships.

God, how long has it been since we've actually seen each other face to face? When will we see each other again? It doesn't matter. You and I: we're good, no matter what.

Pretty much one ourselves, our togetherness doesn't need to be guarded from anything ghosts have to throw at us.

After all, we *are* the ghostly guard.

Note: "The sun has lost its morning brilliance … leaving an afterglow which is easier to bear" (Daphne du Maurier, *Rebecca*).

4434. "an agreeable melancholy"

An agreeable melancholy, which of all the dispositions
of the mind, is the best suited to love and friendship.

Hume, "Of the Delicacy of Taste and Passion"

You're older now: somewhere along the line, you stopped regarding your truest sorrows as injuries that, by the lights of Justice (or in the dark of "just because"), others should remove—or even could.

And besides, you're not sure you really want to part company with those sorrows—at least not forever. You remember the times when sorrow was your only real companion: times when the only thing that could console you for your sorrow was your sorrow itself.

That's the way it always is with true friends. When you're together, there's no one else you'd rather be with.

There's nowhere else you'd rather be.

Note: "the blight man was born for" (Gerard Manley Hopkins, "Spring and Fall: To a Young Child").

4435. Books of Revelation (Class Notes)

> I scarcely know how I know it. The whole train of circumstances seemed to take fire at once, and show it to me.
>
> Dickens, *Our Mutual Friend*

Most of us can tell a plot or a pretense when it crosses our path. (That accent, all that angling—you have got to be kidding! I can read you like a book!)

But there's another book. (Sometimes they're published together in one volume—like two cities in one tale.) It tells the story of the shaky childhood that gave the busy networker his soreness and his start. Or how about that weird-looking girl in school that none of us really noticed? (She must have had her own friends, we figured, real or imagined.) She's in that book too—busy all the time with some bizarre job. It turns out her father was a complete alcoholic and she had to basically support him. (I guess that's why she was such a Class A Biyaatch—impossible to be around, even when you we're trying to be nice.) And then there was that dude (total player) nobody ever remembers seeing sober, but Saved in the

End—saved by the Bell: turns out he wasn't such a dick after all. He really loved that girl whom everyone, even his best friend, was sure he would kick to the curb at the end of the Street. (Someone we know went to the wedding.) Or how about that too-smart-for-her-own-good, sharp-tongued chick, always sullen and snarky, except when some sound of money made her go all soft? Guess what? Chick sort of became a Swan: she ended up with some shady-seeming guy who brought nothing to the table but courage and kindness.

It goes on. It gets better.

So can we.

Note: "And only then she realized that he had a name" (D. H. Lawrence, *The Virgin and the Gipsy*).

"They swept about me and took me up and made me light" ("Our Mutual Friend").

4439. "Dreams advise"

Milton, *Paradise Lost*

Good to know: I could really use some advice but I usually avoid it when I'm awake.

Maybe the only way I can take it now is lying down.

Note: "There is no more activity than passivity" (L. Feuerbach, "On 'The Beginning of Philosophy'").

4441. Over My Head

A *Sunday* hush. Table uncleared. Grandmother
About to take her pill in trembling water
Cocks her head: "An angel's passing over …"
Seeing nothing, each looks at the other.

James Merrill, "Mirabell," *The Changing Light at Sandover*

In the course of clearing the table yesterday morning, to make room for the breakfast she distinctly wanted to make and that I dimly wanted to eat, my mother picked up a book and fell upon the lines that I have quoted above. "I understand that," she said, softly and quickly, awed and augmented by testimony that spelled out what she likes to call a "feeling state," which she (I could tell) has come recently to regard as a familiar spirit. So, you see, the angel (or what you will) passed over twice: first for a Grandmother, and then, years later, for a Mother who read over that first visit. Grandmother and Mother: *they* are the ones who looked at each other in the passage above. As for myself, sensing nothing overhead, what could I do but wonder from the ground at this "supernatural sympathy" (Auden) between someone quite near me and someone quite above me? Where could I be but ready to receive her when she returned to the ground a sentence later? *That reminds me, I need to take my pill.* Why would I admit out loud that soon enough my mother will join her ancestors, and *I* will be the one who stops to salute, between medications, the rumor of their trafficking above?

What can we do right now but continue to act out our daily routines? Right now, my plate's too full with all that she has piled on it, and intends for me to clear, before either of us leaves the table.

Note: "holy hush of ancient" (Wallace Stevens, "Sunday Morning").

AUGUST 2013

206 **4453. "A Need for Gardens" (Richard Brautigan)**

> A poor humanist may possess his soul in patience … admit the energy and brilliancy of the … physical sciences … and still have a happy faith that … men will always require humane letters.
>
> Matthew Arnold, "Literature and Science"

For as long as I have known her, my mother has liked to get very near the works of art that interest her. Once when I was a child, she brought me with her to see some paintings of animals—deer and dogs mostly, as I recall—and I watched her walk up so close to one painting that she could distinguish the individual hairs of its subject, hairs that seemed to have been painted one by one. I thought she was taking some kind of strange, scientific census, like differentiating the leaves of grass that make up a garden or a book of poems. And so she was. But that wasn't all she was doing. Later (much later, I guess—maybe just now, as I started writing this), I figured out that she was up to something else as well. Now I think that all the counting was also her way of conjuring and continuing the animal life that the artist had set out for her to see, and her way of loving him for doing so.

I'm a little sorry it took me so long to get to all this. It's a good thing that certain forms of animal life, like some species of gardens, can go on forever.

And if you really want to find them, you really always can.

Note: "My Grandfather was a minor Washington mystic" (Richard Brautigan, "Revenge of the Lawn").

4454. "Love Enough to Be Kind"

> the class of Grandes Amoureuses, of Women
> Who Love Enough to Be Kind 207
>
> Roland Barthes, *A Lover's Discourse*

—manage to love *enough*, or to love *little* enough to be kind? For a long time I used to be pretty sure it was the latter. For a long time, I used to think that the only love that could be *really* kind (putting someone else's happiness ahead of its own hunger, rather than just pretending to) was something too feeble to care about getting some return (secret or spoken) for all its self-sacrifice. Then I began to wonder whether such not caring shows the strength at least as much as the weakness of the love that will so renounce its own strictly personal interest.

Now I wonder why I ever thought that the difference between such weakness and such strength mattered.

When I was in high school, I had a job at the local library, shelving books. After I went off to college, my mother, who took a hard job to pay for me to go, avoided that library. She kept expecting to see me emerge from the shelves, she told me, and it was more than she could take.

Don't get me wrong. She didn't stop reading. There are other libraries nearby. If she hadn't kept reading, how would she be in a position, even now, to constantly correct me, often long-distance? ("You know history *up to a point*," she's fond of remarking.) Also, as hard as it is for me to really fathom, it turns out that her whole life doesn't actually revolve around me.

Still, though, whenever I pass by that run-down old library, I can't help but catch a glimpse of an eternal archive of the kind of love that will always live for others.

Note: "[She] lived for others" (Gary Wills on his mother).

4456. “without losing his reverence”

> Let a man ... learn to bear the disappearance of things he was wont to reverence, without losing his reverence.
>
> Emerson, “Montaigne; or, The Skeptic”

So much that seemed as solid as a rock just wears down or walks away forever. *I always thought that I'd see you again*, you say to someone who can't hear you—someone you never see anymore.

But then, someone else comes along who *will* see you now, and hear you out.

Sometimes, the best of your love goes not to the person you meant to give it to, but to the one who sees how much you meant to give.

Note: “If my bark sink, 'tis to another se[e]” (William Ellery Channing, “A Poet's Hope,” citation altered).

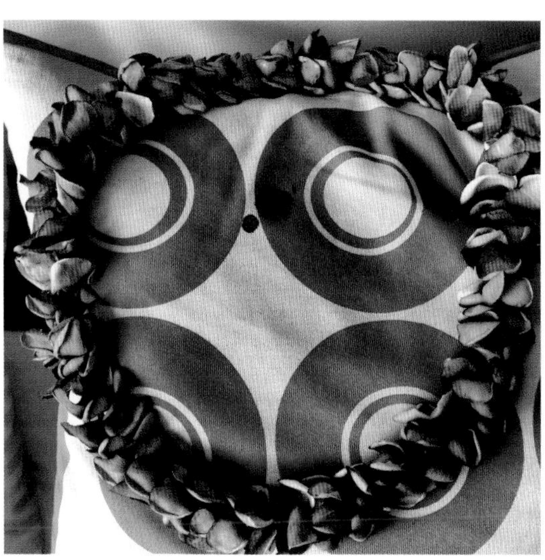

4457. "his sincerities are ... elegiac"

His sincerities are quietly, almost passively elegiac.

Richard Poirier, *The Comic Sense of Henry James*

Personally, I've never met a sincere sentiment that didn't have its root in ground that's pretty much gone now—plowed over and under by some tract-developed cynicism. Just think how old-fashioned most every form of sincerity feel to us—like so many old-school forms of High Society, only something more like the opposite. Even those sincerities uttered by the most recent, thoughtful, individual child may mostly recall to us outmoded selves (ours or others), drowned out by the newer engines of conceit and convention, like the sound of a Grandfather's Mythic Model A, by the speed-of-sound traffic of today's superhighways.

You can't take a picture of this, a boy said to me this summer about the desert sunset of the Southwest, his voice made quiet by the sincere recognition of an evening light that could never be saved. You can't take a picture of this, either: the look on his face as his eyes reckoned with a waning desert light he knew no picture could reproduce.

Still, sincerity itself, even at its most "passively elegiac," even when it's most realized, knowing that it can't save what it wishes with its whole heart that it could, always lays its hearer open to something else: a rumor of a high-fidelity rendering or reprise of some frontier, some future or forgotten ground of openness, always out of reach, but never out of earshot, as near and far as the next true voice you might just hear (never quite here): *Yonder, yes yonder, yonder, ...* (Hopkins, "The Leaden Echo and the Golden Echo").

Note: "What then is the aura? ... the unique apparition of a distance, however near it may be" (W. Benjamin, "The Work of Art in the Age of Technological Reproducibility—Second Version").

4458. "Make gentle the life of this world" (Aeschylus)

> At present, I don't mind confessing … (in strict confidence) that I sometimes find it difficult to keep up a genteel appearance. I have felt the cold here. I have felt something sharper than cold.
>
> Dickens, *Bleak House*

Some nights you wonder what's stronger: the something sharper than any cold that threatens to tear apart all your gentleness, or the someone sweeter in the air who coaxes you to feel confident enough to confess your fear of exposure to such a bleak risk.

And then, by the time you're done choosing your confession, something wonderful has happened *(Who knows how?)* (G. M. Hopkins), but somehow you trust the world enough again to love it. You love the world enough again to trust it. Somehow by some unpredictable advance of keyboard and pen, the scales have turned toward gentleness.

Mirabile dictu: *Sweetness Follows*.

Note: "Live your life filled with joy and thunder" (R.E.M., "Sweetness Follows").

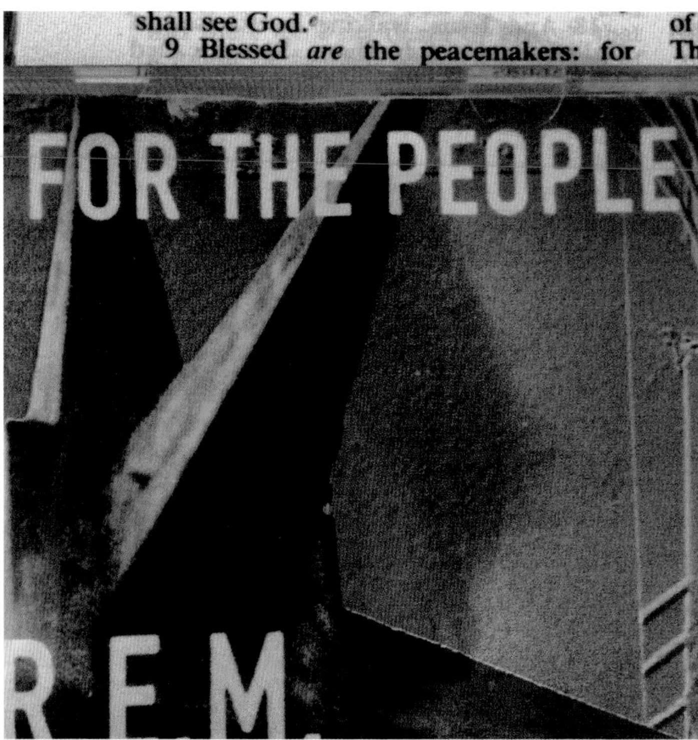

4464. Two Cheers for Vagueness

led by dream and vague desire

Tennyson, "To the Master of Balliol"

If you were to ask me ten years ago what I really wanted and how I wanted it, I'd tell you quicker than a native speaker could say "Sea of Silver" in Spanish. But a lot can happen in ten years. A lot can get clearer and a lot less so. Now, ten years later, I clearly have no clear idea about what I want—only a few clues. One of those clues is that I'm not the only one who feels so confused. When it comes to what I want, I'm pretty sure that there are a lot of people I teach and a lot of people who teach me who are as much out to the foggy sea as I am. (And that sea used to shimmer so!)

Sometimes people are brought together by a common sense that they know what they want (from one another and beyond). Sometimes by a common sense that they don't.

Maybe someday I'll have a clearer feeling of direction. Maybe, someday, I'll decide that all I really want comes down to some annual report of what I've actually done or vaguely dreamed of doing. I can live with that.

You want to know why I can live with that? I'll tell you why I can live with that. Because I think you can live with that, too.

Note:

All I really really want our love to do
Is to bring out the best in me and in you too.
Joni Mitchell, "All I Want"

45742 · 50¢
WASHINGTON SQUARE PRESS
THE Folger Library GENERAL READER'S Shakespeare
Edited by
LOUIS B. WRIGHT and VIRGINIA A. LaMAR
Shakespeare's Sonnets
Illustrated with material in the Folger Library Collections

4465. Continuous Diary

Every liberal-minded man must feel the shame of it.
This is the end. I am not going to keep a diary anymore.

W.N.P. Barbellion on the Treaty of
Versailles, in *A Last Diary* (1919)

But someone else will come along and keep it up, and we both know who that someone else will be. It will be you and I and a lot of people who come after us: that's who it'll be. We're the ones drafted to keep that diary now, the ones determined to cross the gap that no one can cancel. (You know: the gap that spells the differences that divide the States of Men, and the endless destruction of the hope to end all the Wars between them.)

Anyway, ready or not, here we come: *press play*.

Note: "continuingly attentive to the relation of words and deeds, when they seem to become one another" (John Hollander, *The Work of Poetry*).

4466. "But in the movie, died"

... in the book he got the girl
But in the movie, died

John Updike, "In Memoriam"

It's funny where the mind will wander: I wonder if he would have gotten the girl any way at all if he hadn't perished some other way as well. Just think how many people you love had parts that got lost in the shuffle of a move (something shattered, splintered, something stolen away).

And just think how their loss only makes you love them all the more.

Note: "shade of someone lost" (Tennyson, *In Memoriam*).

to write goodbye now so I
you have lent me in spite
The receiver4 is mutable
solution parce que il n'y
baby do da do da The light

personal correspondence

4468. "It's the kingdom of heaven"

> There always comes a moment when people give up struggling and tearing each other apart, willing at last to like each other for what they are. It's the kingdom of heaven.
>
> Camus, *Notebooks*

It's like a great scene in some movie about accepting a mermaid, where Tom Hanks asks John Candy what he thinks about women running around naked through the streets of

New York. *I'm for it of course*, Candy replies. Hard not to get happy after a line like that: hard to be hard on the dude who delivers himself of this sentiment: hard not to feel the line of the laugh extend to forgive the one who laughs as well as the one who is laughed at.

That's terrible, my mother will say while she's laughing her head off at some bawdy comedy.

It's her way of telling that she's as close as she'll come to heaven on earth.

Note:

> natural sinners put him at his ease,
> And so he enters the cathedral door.
> (Witter Bynner, "Santa Fe")

4474. "the small band of true friends"

> the small band of true friends …
> the perfect happiness of the union
>
> Jane Austen, *Emma*

My mother and I seldom speak of heaven. Neither of us imagine that we have any idea of what it would be like. Last night, though, in the middle of our usual conversation, the subject unexpectedly arose. I said that as far as I could tell, what people mostly mean by heaven is some place where they get to be with friends and family who are gone now: that for many people, it wasn't so much a strict belief as a dim hope for such a get-together. This conjured an image in her mind of all of the dogs she'd ever had (she's had a lot), starting when she was a little girl. As she began to name them (the list sounded a little like Santa's Reindeer Roster, only a few of the names forgotten), her voice roved away from the voice that I know as her voice, as if it were following the band of dogs to some place far from here. "I think they would all get along," she said, a little shyly.

How could I help but believe her?

Note: "Hatted, as for departure, away from us … sometimes talking, sometimes not, always in conversation" (Stanley Cavell, "Adam's Rib," *Pursuits of Happiness: The Hollywood Comedy of Remarriage*).

4477. "The end of art is peace"

> The end of art is peace
> Could be the motto of this frail device.
>
> Seamus Heaney, "The Harvest Bow"

So true. It's also the place where sickness and anger, and all their ugly memories, finally come to reach an understanding. (When you're peaceful enough, what you'll remember about your father are the good times: like when he tried his bashful best to show you how to use some tool for gardening or just getting along.)

Your father and his tools: here's a Parable, a Paradox, from our own backyard: all those things that he tried to show you how to use (lawn mowers, long dividers, and the like)—they seem more useful now that they've been tossed from the toolshed: just lying there, exposed to the elements, their edges worn away, his rusty implements reveal themselves, for what they really are at last, in the reflected light of his love.

Note: "swords into plowshares" (Isaiah 2:4).

4478. "our Puritan anxiety"

... our Puritan anxiety to "do ye next thing"

Anne Morrow Lindbergh, *Gift from the Sea*

What's next, you always worry. What do I have to do next, and if I don't do it, what will be done to *me*? What have I already done to ruin everything—*what have I done? what have I done?*

Sometimes when the fear gets thick enough, life just feels like one long "to-do" list. You get going and pretty soon you're running around in circles and you don't know where to start or where to stop.

But wait: maybe the thing your worry really wants you to do right now is to quit *doing* things (fighting wars, flying planes, finding ways, etc.) for right now, and just spend a little quality time with it.

I mean, it's like with any other good friend. You should enjoy him while you can. He always has a lot of good things to say if you just hear him out and sometimes read between his lines. He's not just barking orders. He's also bearing gifts. And it's not like he can hang around forever—just until you've unwrapped the presents that he's brought you from a long way overseas.

Note: "a spirit of courage, and wisdom and zeal" (Thomas Shepard Jr., "Eye Salve," *The Puritans in America: A Narrative Anthology*, ed. Alan Heimert and Andrew Delbanco).

alley, and
l Villains.
rits high.

Once upon the Sandwich Isles,
the social structure steamed upon Hawaii.
Rock, rock, roll Plymouth Rock roll over.

SEPTEMBER 2013

4479. "Nature's first green is gold"

Nature's first green is gold,
Her hardest hue to hold.

Robert Frost, "Nothing Gold Can Stay"

Isn't that just the way with most hues held dear? Hard to tell sometimes: Not knowing they're going before they go is a regular part of the deal.

Note: "The tendre croppes" (Chaucer, "The General Prologue").

4481. "her lovely, deliberate blandness"

When Eleanor Roosevelt came to see [JFK] at the White House, he insisted that she allow him to show her her old home. As they were about to leave his office, he motioned for her to precede him through the door. Mrs. Roosevelt drew back. "No," she said. "You go first. You are the President."

He laughed. "I keep forgetting." With her lovely, deliberate blandness, she replied, "But you must never forget."

Gore Vidal on Eleanor Roosevelt,
"John Kennedy: A Translation for the English"

What are we to make of this parable? Well, for one thing, this: when we occupy offices where we are responsible for setting an example (President, Teacher, Citizen, Mother, Minister, Mentor), we should never entirely forget that responsibility, even when we want to, and even when we think no one else is looking. Setting an example for others requires constant and consistent practice. Setting an example for others requires constant and consistent regard for a standard of character larger and higher than our individual selves.

I gather this is what Mrs. Roosevelt sought to remind the glamorous and insouciant-seeming young man who had assumed a position of indisputably awesome influence.

But I do not think the teaching stops there. For those of us enamored by what appeals to our eyes because it appears to be the opposite of blandness—signature-making surface styles of quickness, sharpness, and shimmer—there is another lesson to be learned, one that relates to and reinforces the first. That lesson is this: a force of charisma may adhere to the most conventional-seeming people and propositions, a force that renders vivid and vivacious the particular personality of the person and the proposition at the very moment when it is most concerned with constituting itself as nothing more than the conveyor of a commonplace—*her lovely, deliberate blandness.*

Her lovely, deliberate blandness: Mrs. Roosevelt neither sought nor gained a reputation as a clothes horse. Still, I cannot help but hear, in this phrase that so admires her, the love of a poet at the sight of his girl in silks. There she is, somehow surpassing, while fully inhabiting, the splendid but, for its day, standard fashion she has put on—there she is, *that brave vibration each way free* (Herrick, "Upon Julia's Clothes").

Note: “Thus fashion represents nothing more than one of many forms of life by ... which we seek to combine ... the tendency towards social equalization with the desire for individual differentiation” (G. Simmel, “Fashion”).

4483. "Men who die childless ... are denied an ancestor shrine"

... only those who have children born to their name

Jack Goody, *Death, Property and the Ancestors: A Study of the Mortuary Customs of the Lodagaa of West Africa*

You know what? I can live with that. Not everyone in the whole, wide world needs an ancestor shrine—which is just as well, since, given the scarcity of space, there probably isn't room enough for everyone in the whole wide world to have one. (I have to think this is especially true, nowadays, what with women's lib and changes in eligibility requirements, the number of ancestors entitled to shrines has greatly increased. And the situation can only get worse: There's probably some mathematical formula to figure out the proportions of the possible proliferation of shrines, but I'm no good at math. Still, even I can see how the world could get so overpopulated with them that you wouldn't be able to get across the street to get a cup of coffee or something, without tripping over a few. It could be a real problem.)

So, like I say: not having an ancestor shrine: I'm fine with that. The way I see it, I'll get lost in the crowd instead. (I've always loved a crowd.)

I'll be lost in the crowd.

And found there as well.

Note: "Men can die without anxiety if they know that what they love is protected from misery and oblivion" (Herbert Marcuse, *Eros and Civilization*).

4490. "For our vines have tender grapes"

> O my dove, that art in the clefts of the rock, in the secret places of the stairs, let me see thy countenance, let me hear thy voice; for sweet is thy voice, and thy countenance is comely. Take us the foxes, the little foxes, that spoil the vines: for our vines have tender grapes.
>
> Song of Solomon 2:14–15

I used to be afraid that the things I loved (the poems and the people I somehow thought could make my dreams come true), I loved too hard. And I was right to be afraid: there was a drive to argue embedded in my loving, a drive hard enough to smash and spoil whatever sweetness lay in the original intent. I got into so many Huge, High Arguments over what I loved, and got so into winning those arguments, that I didn't even notice, until it was too late, that I had laid to waste the tender feelings I was arguing over—like destroying a village in order to save it.

I'd like to think that's mostly over now (along with the dream of most dreams coming true). Now I want to try to tend to what I love in ways less intent on *getting* something out of them (more involved with *giving* something to them).

Who knows what crops will come back once the desert foxes have been laid to rest?

Note: "My fall knocked a mean chip out of me" (R.E.M.).

4492. "Sincerity"

> Sincerity is an essential part of his method of depicting his own random life in its entirety.
>
> Erich Auerbach on Montaigne, "L'Humaine Condition," *Mimesis: The Representation of Reality in Western Literature*

You start out saying you'll stay true to a lot of things: your flag, your friends, your family, your finer self. And you do an okay job doing so, but *let's face it*, as my mother always says. (By the way, that's one of her favorite formulas: I wonder where she was the first time she said it; I wonder to whom she said it, that first time, and why. Maybe she was breaking up with a boyfriend—like the guy from Colville, Washington, who stood her up at the high school homecoming where she was crowned queen. "Oh, he had some feeble excuse, but I cooled on him after that," she says. It makes me think of a few feeble excuses I've made myself—okay, maybe more than a few—ah, *but I digress*).

Anyway, let's face it, when it comes to staying true, we fail as much as we succeed. We try to be faithful where we've offered our faith, but things change so fast (or so slowly) that we don't even notice all we've forgotten—sometimes it feels like almost everything. (It's like what my father always used to say, before he forgot to say it: "I've already forgotten twice as much as what you know.")

Sometimes keeping a promise to stay in touch proves as hard as governing hormones or harmony or your power to hear a call for help. Keeping a promise to stay in touch can be as tricky as staying on a single subject in a sentence or an essay whose only intention is to let someone know that we want to be in touch with him. We meant—well … we meant well.

Then sincerity comes to save the connections. Like charity, being true begins at home, and brings us back there, too. *To thine own self be true:* and just by being so, you're true to others as well.

Then even *I'm sorry, I can't be with you* means in some way you can.

Then every departure can be a way of staying near.

Note: "I hope that my study will reach its readers. ... And may it contribute to bringing together again those whose love for our ... history has serenely persevered" (Auerbach, "Epilogue," *Mimesis*).

4493. "Fallings from us, vanishings"

... for these I raise
The song of thanks and praise;
... for those obstinate questionings
Of sense and outward things,
Fallings from us, vanishings;
Blank misgivings of a Creature
Moving about in worlds not realized,
High instincts before which our mortal Nature
Did tremble like a guilty thing surprised.

Wordsworth, "Ode: Intimations of Immortality from Recollections of Early Childhood"

For *these*? *Really*? For these offshore, extralegal, totally unreviewable interrogations I'm supposed to feel grateful? My God! *Really?*

I get how I'm supposed to be grateful and praise all the livelong day. It's like what an Indian friend said to me in graduate school. I was talking about how I felt "sorry" for some professor. I'm not sure I really felt sorry for him, but it seemed like a good thing to say at the time. "Why? He's got a wife. He's got kids. He's got a job. He's got a house. He's got a car. Why do you feel sorry for him?" Now *I'm* a professor, and I get how I should probably be down on my knees thanking and praising every day of the week and twice on Sunday, and never be feeling sorry for myself. Well, the truth is that I *do* thank and praise a lot. And here's a further truth: I *am* raising the song of thanks and praise, *especially* when I've been feeling sorry for myself.

Let me put it this way. I don't know what goes on for you when you first wake up in the morning. (The truth is that I don't know what goes on for anyone else when he or she first wakes up in the morning. I didn't, even when I regularly saw someone else when he or she first woke up in the morning, and I certainly don't now that it's been longer than I can remember since I saw someone else when he or she first woke up in the morning.) So like I say, I don't know how you feel when you first wake up in the morning, but I can tell you how I feel: Sad. Lonely. In the dark. Fearful that I've missed out on some natural nearness or vague dearness and nagged by the suspicion that I once had those things and somehow lost them and, to top it all off, am helpless to stop the questions about *how* I lost them.

It used to be so easy between us that there didn't even feel like there was anything between us, and now I'm second-guessing every last conversation we have. What's up with that? Do I really have to go and ruin everything I touch—everything that touches me?

And by the way, what's with all the questions? *Who's* with all the questions? These questions that have my heart in some kind of lock when I first wake up: are they *my* questions, or are they brought to me by someone else from far away, whom I am somehow made to serve as a vessel and a voice? And who is that "special someone" with all the questions? Are we related? Are you, by any chance, my *father* (Mr. *Mad-Man-*Math), practically a ghost now, coming at me with yet another "prisoner's dilemma" type problem, just like you did when I was young? Only this time it's even *more* vague than it was back in the day—one more missed "gift" of knowledge that just keeps on *taking* (sorry! I mean *giving*, of course)! *Thank. You. Dad!* I didn't understand what the *hell* you were trying to teach me then, and I sure as *hell* don't understand now, what with all the value and visible signs removed.

(Blank misgivings of a Creature
Moving about in worlds not realized
High instincts before which our mortal Nature
Did tremble like a guilty thing surprised)

And by the way, since you're on me again, in the original contract, aren't *you* the one who's supposed to *tremble like a guilty and surprised*? Last I checked, *you're* it, all ghostly and imprisoned and whipped:

And then it started like a guilty thing
Upon a fearful summons.
(*Hamlet*, describing the ghost of the Father)

Where was I when the vote got called to saddle *my team* with the guilt-project? *There's* a memo I missed! I mean I know how we're supposed to *own our work* and all (I *hate* that consultant-firm cliché, by the way—so managerial and *manipulative*), but since when is feeling guilty *my* work? *What the F—*

Wait. Just stop. Enough with all the obstinacy, already. We could prosecute the precedents six ways to Sunday. But let's not. Look. Whoever you are, whoever I am, I and my mortal nature both—we're sorry for all the misunderstandings. And we're glad and grateful to have you back, even with all the pondering pain and confusion. My mortal nature and I, we wake up every morning feeling like we lost something big. So, I gather, Mr. Big-Boss, do you. Let's team up together. Let's call a truce.

Let's call it a day.

Note: "morning's minion" (Hopkins, "The Windhover").

5002. "Love those for whom the world is real"

However seldom in my line to feel,
I most love those for whom the world is real.

James Merrill, "The Book of Ephraim,"
The Changing Light at Sandover

"This is really something," a girl said last night, about the strange ceramic clown that has been part of my household for years. As alarmingly self-satisfied as the clown looks, I just know that he's anything but. (I assume it's a he, though I can't say for sure: its gender does not submit to simple identification.)

If my young guest and her friends hadn't been considerate enough to celebrate his existence, I just know that my poor clown would have spent the night (as he has spent many nights) in a state of darkness about his very being.

That clown is a parable: Think how often you and I cast about in shadows, unsure of our own being, not feeling it, no matter how game our face, like so many sad and lonely clowns or clouds or crowds, until someone quick and bright comes along to draw it out.

Where would we be without those special someones to confirm our especial existence?

Lucky for us, they're no further away than the next real surprise.

Note: "a world which has meaning only for a consciousness" (Hazel Barnes, "Humanistic Existentialism and Contemporary Psychoanalysis," *The Literature of Possibility: A Study of Humanistic Existentialism*).

5007. "Then, all of a sudden, I started to cry"

> Then, all of a sudden, I started to cry. I couldn't help it. I did it so nobody could hear me, but I did it. It scared hell out of old Phoebe when I started doing it, and she came over and tried to make me stop, but once you get started, you can't just stop on a goddamn *dime*.
>
> J. D. Salinger, *The Catcher in the Rye*

My best friend likes to brag that his father, a truck driver who left when everyone involved was young, could park a semi on a *dime*. He says it a lot because, like me, he's not exactly the type of person who could park any kind of vehicle on a *dime*, goddamn or otherwise, and it makes him feel proud to be related to someone who could.

On the other hand, my best friend knows how to live with the fact that there's no way of knowing when a lot of what moves us will come to a serious stop. (I mean a full stop—some final calm, some kingdom come.)

Meanwhile, though, he pulls over when he needs to rest and plugs what meters he can.

Believe me, he has plenty of change.

Note: *Lacrimae rerum* (Virgil).

5008. "a God to thank"

I have never wished there was a God to call on—I have often wished for a God to thank.

F. Scott Fitzgerald, *The Notebooks*

My father's mother practiced some brand of Buddhism she picked up and polished over the course of a long life of working hard and feeling right. Every morning and every night, she'd go to her homemade shrine and clap her hands and produce offerings. This was how she called the Chief, she explained to me. I must have found her calling interesting, because I started doing it, too. Over and over and over again. "Dial it down," she told me, in the mix-and-match blended language we spoke to each other: "He's a busy guy and can only visit each caller twice a day."

Well, like they say, the Pilgrim doesn't fall far from the Shrine. Now, every morning, the grandson wakes up determined to call someone very far away. He wants to be in touch with a distant someone to whom he can confess his confusion or some other part of his commotion. Everyone's gotten busier, so he only acts on the urge once a day now. As far as offerings go, instead of rice, he's got a mess of words and pictures requisitioned from the stockpiles he's harvested over the years.

During the call, that descendant talks about a lot of different things (maybe it's practice for all the talking he'll be doing later; maybe it's penance for all the talking he's already done).

That said, there's really only one thing that he wants to get across to anyone who may be hearing or overhearing him. Thanks for taking me in: *Thanks for that.*

I hope to do the same for someone, someday.

Maybe today.

Note: "Whoever you are, I have always depended on the kindness of strangers" (Tennessee Williams, *A Streetcar Named Desire*).

OCTOBER 2013

234 5012. It's Different from the Ones in Peru

> No age is so apt as youth to think its emotions, partings, and resolves are the last of their kind. Each crisis seems final, simply because it is new. We are told that the oldest inhabitants in Peru do not cease to be agitated by the earthquakes, but they probably see beyond each shock, and reflect that there are plenty more to come.
>
> George Eliot, *Middlemarch*

Once you get to be one of those old-timers in Peru, though, new agitations, different from your first earthquakes, come along to threaten your peace.

Remember the first time you knew for sure that the person you thought you'd make a life with had pulled his stakes out of the grounds you shared? Remember that? *Of course I d[o] ... it almost broke my heart* (Virginia Woolf, *Mrs. Dalloway*).

Remember how we survived that one? You don't? Neither do I. But we did, just the same, and here we are now to talk about it.

But wait: that's not what we're here to talk about. Now it's something else that promises to pull the ground out from under us. That's what we're here to talk about: the latest thing to shock our world.

But wait: we can't talk about that yet. It's hard to talk in the middle of an earthquake (especially a new one: you don't know where the tremors are coming from or how large they'll get or how long they'll last). It's hard to talk about an unclear and present danger.

Just you wait, though: sooner or later the dust will settle, and we'll live to tell the tale.

At least, as much as we can.

Note: "Consent, with as much courage as Plotinus did, to every dimension of human experience, and to everything within it that is mysterious, inexpressible, and transcendent" (Pierre Hadot, *Plotinus, or, The Simplicity of Vision*).

5014. "I cannot be mended"

Wallace Stevens, "Idiom of the Hero"

—but I sure can be moved.

Note: "befriended" ("Idiom of the Hero").

5016. "Where every paradox means wonder"

Nearer to that green lake
Where every paradox means wonder.

James Merrill, "The Black Swan"

It's like the way you feel sometimes when you first wake up in the morning, still wet from some plunging dream. You're a little older and a little younger. You've let people down and you've given them a lift, all on one drive. You feel more lonely and loved by the minute. You have infinite hope, not for yourself, but you hope for someone else. You're nothing but mistaken and still true to the mission. You feel more fright and more fortitude than you ever possibly thought you could feel all at once. You're sure you've seen everything and you're sure that everything remains to be unhidden.

You're ready to start the day.

Note: "the song of me rising from bed and meeting the sun" (Whitman, "Song of Myself").

5017. Self-Pastoral

> The quick vision that his life was after all a failure.
>
> George Eliot, *Middlemarch*

Then the curing vision that it's not: on those days when you're convinced that you're pretty much a total fool, consider the people you might have helped to hope that they themselves don't have to be.

Note: "catechize you under that name" (*Middlemarch*).

5018. "how he got out of the room"

> Deronda did not know how he got out of the room.
>
> George Eliot, *Daniel Deronda*

If he knew, he'd tell you. Maybe's he a little stiff, but basically he's a sweet guy, and if he could give you a map or a manual that would show you how to pass through the most painful parting, I'm sure he would.

Meanwhile, though, he wanted me to tell you something (he comes to me sometimes in my sleep). What did he want me to tell you? I'm not exactly sure, now. Something about how there's always someone waiting to tell you something. It could be something big.

I'm pretty sure you'll be able to hear it better once you're out of the room.

5019. The Strangeness of Tears

—he struck her as confessing with strange tears in his own eyes, to sharp identity of emotion.

H. James, *The Golden Bowl*

I guess the secret to receiving a confession like that is to avoid thinking you know its secret before you do. Just because you've heard someone's name, rank, and serial number doesn't mean you can tell right away where he's from or where he's going. The same goes for tears: no matter how much they make themselves at home with you, they'll always take their orders from some secret ministry you'll never see.

Given all the advances in transport that make the world smaller every day, it's good to know that there's still someplace so far away.

Note: "religious mysticism proper" (William James, *The Varieties of Religious Experience*).

5024. "We are going to be in for trouble"

David: Mama. We are going to be in for trouble. You understand that?

Fanny: I understand it very well. We will manage. You and I. I'm not put together with flour paste. And neither are you—I am happy to learn.

Lillian Hellman, *Watch on the Rhine*

A day doesn't go by that I don't partly spend worried to the point of distraction about *something*. If it's not about something I said, it's about something I didn't say. If it's not some blemish I see in the mirror, which I'm sure means the further degradation of whatever it is that makes me fit to be seen, it's a blemish in my field of vision, which I am sure means the further failure of my fitness to see.

If it's not the fear that I've lost or will soon lose someone I love, it's the fear of the loss of the world that I share with those I love or have loved.

I'll tell you about a day when I wasn't fearful, though, at least not that I can remember—thirteen days, actually. Many things terrify a four-year-old, but one thing that didn't terrify me when *I* was four years old was the Cuban Missile Crisis, though it might well have, since it took place shortly after my fourth birthday, and I was fully prepared by then to be scared by anything that proposed itself for me to fear. My mom and dad sure were scared. "We thought it really might be the end of the world," my mother told me later. But she didn't tell me that then. I don't remember her saying anything unusual, anything that stood out from the usual carousel of practical, moral, and intellectual instructions that made my early childhood one long, repeated lesson in Self-Improvement.

I wonder if she knew that the example of her self-restraint was the most important lesson of all.

Note: "You have to accept whatever comes and the only important thing is that you meet it with courage and the best that you have to give" (Eleanor Roosevelt to Edward R. Murrow).

5025. "where nobody was looking"

He liked finding things where nobody was looking.

Susan Sontag on Walter Benjamin, "Under the Sign of Saturn"

Same here. I like finding things where nobody was looking—me included. There I was, my head buried in some old book or bad mood, and suddenly, when I was least expecting it, someone came along and took me to the place I was looking to go. Strange: I didn't even know I was looking to go there until I actually got there.

It's like the way the most labored sentence (*hard labor!*) suddenly gets commuted by some simple phrase whose sole power is to set you free.

There you go!

Note: "all the places I got found" (Coldplay, "Speed of Sound")

5026. Coming up Empty

The inexpressive haunts and even hollows these poems.

John Updike, "Christian Verse"

It looks to me like one of those half-empty, half-full situations—the hollowness you feel when you first wake up: *hallowed be thy name.*

Note: "The central hollowness" (James Merrill, "The Black Swan").

5027. "It was now too late and too far to go back"

> We changed again, and yet again, and it was now too late and too far to go back, and I went on.
>
> Dickens, *Great Expectations*

He's just learning the first lesson of growing up: you have to hurry your good-byes or you'll never really leave, and once you really leave you can never really go back. The second lesson is figuring out how rules are made to be broken.

Note: “Have you escaped, sir, the Locked Door policy?” (from a dream of E. M. Forster).

brother (boyhood)

5030. "note"

It was with sincere modesty that I called it a "note."

Roland Barthes, "From Taste to Ecstasy"

—modesty, and a moving sense (a sense that's moved me anyway) that anything I write may be the last thing I ever write.

It's like what old people are forever telling young people, one way or another: when you part company with someone, just imagine that you are parting from him forever.

You give him your best and you hope for the best—it's the same best that someone, just before you never heard from him again, somehow gave to you.

Note: "One might … speak of an unforgettable life or moment even if all men had forgotten it" (Walter Benjamin, "The Task of the Translator").

5032. "where lost was found"

… here in final state, where lost was found

James Merrill, "The Will"

That's what it feels like as we sail into some final phase of a season or a sonnet or a song or a swan or a sermon or a swell or a swelling or a sentence or a—well, you get the idea (it's an idea of something beyond the Endless Summer sound of a single consonant).

There's something I've been meaning to tell you, or that you've been meaning to tell me, something forgotten along the way. It's like how at the end of *Moby-Dick*, the narrator finally gets around to telling the families (he sure takes the long way) that their sons and fathers and husbands have been lost at sea. (Turns out that was his task all along: who knew? He sure didn't tell us. Talk about getting off message!) Finally, though, in the end, he remembers what he's come to report. He starts the last chapter of a book as big as the Bible, practically—it could have been as brief as one of those telegrams from the War Office—by quoting the servant who comes to tell Job that what he loves has been all destroyed: *And I only am escaped alone to tell thee* (Job 1:15; *Moby-Dick*, "Epilogue"), and then he goes on to say that all that's left are orphans.

How did I get on this again? Oh yeah: how in the end what got lost along the way will be found. We all get so didactic or otherwise distracted and detached sometimes, but in the end we remember what we forgot.

Or we find something better.

Note: "I always cry at endings" (Belle and Sebastian).

[129] William Blake's poetry and writings provide a commentary on
[130] These overlapping images from Genesis and Revelation also for
Earthly Paradise, in Dante's *Divine Comedy* (*Purgatorio*, xxx–xxxiii),
counters Beatrice.

5033. Loving on Time

Ave Maria! 'tis the hour of Love!

Byron, *Don Juan*, Third Canto

Sometimes, after the hour has passed, you still want to talk about it.

Then you wind up loving the ones (their own hour still to come) willing to hear a little about the hour that's passed.

Love changes hands. That's how it lasts.

Note: "that face so fair!" (*Don Juan,* Third Canto).

5034. "lost for lacke of telling"

Here is a great deale of good matter,
lost for lacke of telling.

Spenser, "Julye," *The Shepheardes Calendar*

Sometimes I worry that my mother tells me her stories too often. (It's surely a sign of old age.) Do you have any idea how many times I've heard how "Old Man Tannenbaum (sp.?)" got separated from the rest of his hunting party, but had the good sense to light a fire and stay put until his friends came to rescue him?

Sometimes I worry that she can't tell them often enough.

Note: "Still to recall, to praise" (James Merrill, "Christmas Tree").

5035. Thanks for That

For this relief much thanks.

Shakespeare, *Hamlet*

Can you imagine a book that would catalog every human kindness? Neither can I. And we both know why. It's because no one could ever say much about the best things that people do for one another—they're too large or too small (largely, too small). You can never really define them. The strength that people help send your way: well, that's as much beyond your power to measure as the weight of the weaknesses that it works a little to lighten. And the feeling that others, near and far, bring you (so many Messages, so many Messengers!)—the feeling of being with someone else: that's as much beyond all telling as the loneliness that this feeling puts a little to rest. It's kind of like what some philosophers say about Evil (how it eludes all efforts to comprehend it), only equal and opposite.

Well, anyway, all I really want so say is all anyone *can* say, under the circumstances: Thanks for that.

Thanks for that.

Note: "that surpasses all understanding" (Philippians 4:7).

5039. “so right”

> Now beyond the reach of scandal, his best writing validated by time, he comes before us still, a towering figure, laughing and weeping, with parables and paradoxes, so generous, so amusing, and so right.
>
> Richard Ellmann, *Oscar Wilde*

Actually, he was wrong a lot. In fact, he was wrong most of his time. Being wrong was what made his Clubhouse famous. Infamous, more like: it’s what brought him down.

He was wrong to believe that being witty would always save him from the worst: wrong to think that those taken in by his charm would take him in when he had nowhere else to go: wrong to imagine that his sayings would make people wonder so much that they would exempt him from every rule, grammatical and ingrained.

But here’s the best way he was wrong: He really believed that if he just talked quickly enough he could bring everyone over to his side: the un-blind side: the side where everyone gets to play.

Sometimes when you lose the Game on errors, you wind up winning in the end.

Note: “Oscar Wilde was always right” (Borges, “About Oscar Wilde”).

5040. Street-Level Closeness

Only from me can they hide nothing.

Whitman, "The Sleepers," *Leaves of Grass*

—but only when they're sure that there's nothing I can hide from them.

Of course, this rule of reciprocal disclosure only applies to those of us who failed the test to become a secret agent or an old-school confessor (the types behind a curtain or a screen, iron or ironic, or something in between). Those types: *wow!* It's like you have to tell them *everything* since they're not telling you *anything* and *somebody* has to be giving *something* up to *someone*, pretty much all the time. That's just the way the world works. It's some general law of circulation or hydraulics discovered in the Renaissance or thereabouts. (I'm probably not explaining it well, but you know what I mean.)

Speaking of the way the world works, have you ever noticed how a kid will sometimes show you her angel side, but only when she's sure that you really need to know it?

Note: "no white-winged angels now … [b]ut … a hand … which leads … forth gently towards a calm and bright land … the hand may be a … child's" (George Eliot, *Silas Marner*).

NOVEMBER 2013

5042. Waiting for Light

In a place of blackness,
Here I stay and wait.

Stephen Crane, "The Black Riders and Other Lines"

When it's dark around you, shouldn't you get up and go where it's light? Isn't that always the right thing to do?

Sometimes, though, if you wait in the dark for a while, the light will eventually come to you.

Note: "Patience" (Milton, on his blindness).

5043. Playing Fair with Your Feelings

> Young John lay wrapt in peaceful slumber, after composing and arranging the following monumental inscription on his pillow.
>
> Dickens, *Little Dorrit*

You can read the inscription in a second. (I've laid it out below.) You've probably already produced some version of it yourself: It's the script that we write in our heads where we re-cast our own personal, passing hurt into a drama fit for the Ages. Most of those scripts are so over the top that we take one glance at them and toss them on the reject-pile. There's that ridiculous story, for example, of some bruised loser-dude who thinks he's been crowned the King of Pain just because some pretty girl has said no to him and yes to someone else.

But you shouldn't throw those scripts out without a fair reading. (Think of it this way: Just because you can see right through someone doesn't always mean you should.) Most of the time, of course, taking your own feelings too seriously means that you're not taking other people's feelings seriously enough. On the other hand, casting yourself as the king of pain every once in a while can prompt you to act a little like a prince to other men.

Note: "for the sake of the loved" (*Little Dorrit*).

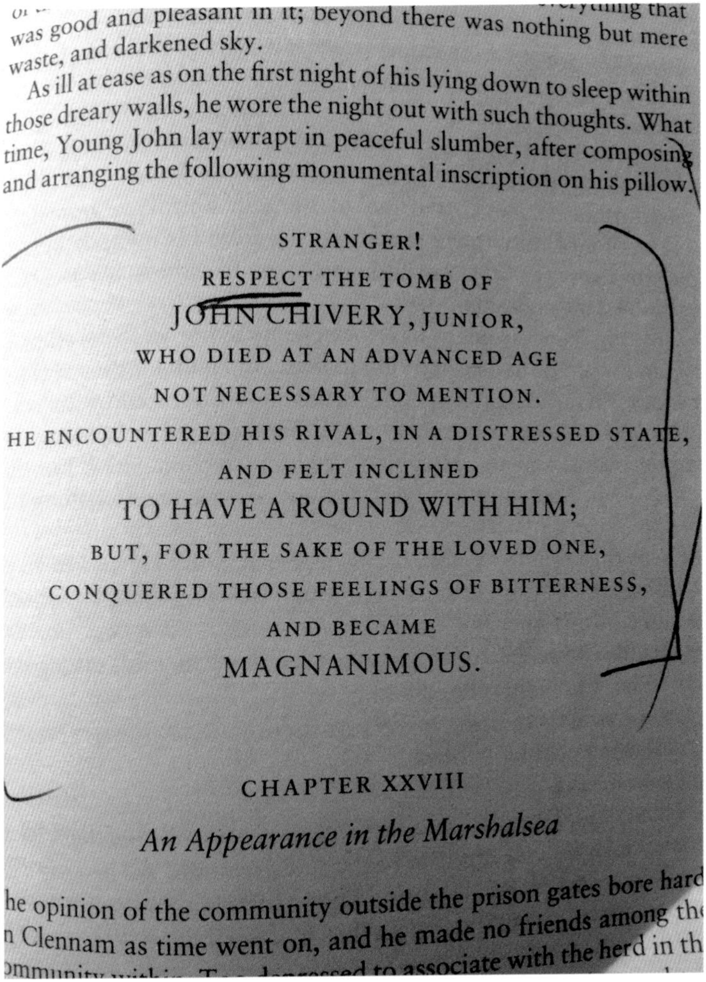

was good and pleasant in it; beyond there was nothing but mere waste, and darkened sky.

As ill at ease as on the first night of his lying down to sleep within those dreary walls, he wore the night out with such thoughts. What time, Young John lay wrapt in peaceful slumber, after composing and arranging the following monumental inscription on his pillow.

STRANGER!
RESPECT THE TOMB OF
JOHN CHIVERY, JUNIOR,
WHO DIED AT AN ADVANCED AGE
NOT NECESSARY TO MENTION.
HE ENCOUNTERED HIS RIVAL, IN A DISTRESSED STATE,
AND FELT INCLINED
TO HAVE A ROUND WITH HIM;
BUT, FOR THE SAKE OF THE LOVED ONE,
CONQUERED THOSE FEELINGS OF BITTERNESS,
AND BECAME
MAGNANIMOUS.

CHAPTER XXVIII

An Appearance in the Marshalsea

he opinion of the community outside the prison gates bore hard n Clennam as time went on, and he made no friends among the ommunity within. Too depressed to associate with the herd in the

5044. "(I too in this dictum)"

> If only one person were capable of leaving off one word before the truth! Everyone (I too in this dictum) overruns truth by hundreds of words.
>
> Kafka, "Fragments from Note-Books and Loose Pages," *Wedding Preparations in the Country*

254 Truer words were never spoken, and I think I know why. I think we all do, actually, though it's one of the few things we don't like to talk about too much.

Of course we talk too much (certainly past Truth's Finish Line). We need our words to keep ourselves together. How could we weave our dumb drive to *be together*, without our words? (It would be like running without socks, or on a wounded Achilles: neither ever a good idea.)

No wonder my mother repeats herself so much. "Oh, I know I repeat myself, but I figure if I tell the same thing two or three times to the same person, I've doubled or tripled the number of my friends." Two or three times? Try twenty or thirty thousand times!—wait: have I already told you she said that? What can I say? I guess the best defense against the prospect of no friends is a strong offense (I too in this repeated dictation).

I mean, what's the truth if not the end of all that we've got going on together here? (Maybe there's more to it than that. I sure hope so: but it's like what the Philosopher says: that about which we cannot speak, we must pass over in silence. He's says it in German, and I've yet to see a translation that's not awkward to enunciate. That's why you say it over and over again. You keep thinking: this time, it'll come out right. It's like the great line—the greatest—from the New Testament: *For unto whomsoever much is given, of him shall be much required*. Try saying that ten times. I mean it: *Try it*.)

Anyway, like I was saying: before the Door of the Truth, what would the last word be except, except [...], and let me tell you something, I have no intention of saying *that* word—not without a fight, anyway. It makes me think of a girl I knew in graduate school who decided she hated my guts and was all set to dissolve our friendship, but then thought about all the conversations she'd have to have with me about her decision: "All those lunches! All that processing! All those talks to get to the bottom of the problem!" (She decided in the end that ending it just wasn't worth the trouble. Wise woman. Good choice. Good choice.)

Funny story, right? I can be a very determined person. Speaking of determination, my brother and I were talking on the phone last night, congratulating ourselves about how right and determined we are, unlike kids these days. (You'd think *we* were the ones who had grown up during the Depression, rather than our parents. It's like what a friend said to me the other night: "We didn't grow up during the Depression. We just grew up *depressed*").

I've told you about my brother, haven't I? He's super straight (Old-School Straight), but not exactly the silent type. He talks as much as I do. Well, almost as much, anyway. Garrulousness and thinking we're always right aren't the only things we share, incidentally. Sometimes we also watch soccer on TV together. (It's true, we watch for different reasons, but the important thing is that we're together, right?) Anyway, I was talking to my brother on the phone tonight—by the way, speaking of brothers and stories, have you heard the one about the poet whose brother dies and he (the surviving brother, I mean) has to run halfway around the world to visit the grave? Actually, that's pretty much the whole story—not much of a story, come to think of it. There's not a lot more to say. Well, there one more thing to say, but I'm not saying it. Let someone else talk, for a change. It's like what Erving Goffman (greatest sociologist *ever*—he's all over the weird ways that people go along to get along) supposedly said at his wife's funeral: *today someone else will have to take the notes*.

In any case, like I say, *I'm* not saying it.

Not yet, anyway.

Note: *in perpetuum, frater, ave atque vale* (Catullus, 101).

5045. Coming and Going

> How banal
> Our lives would be, how shrunken, but for you.
>
> James Merrill, *The Changing Light at Sandover*

With you around, there's always so much to do: all that getting ready to say good-bye.

All that getting ready to say hello.

Note: *Aloha.*

5047. Another Country

I drew a map of Canada
Oh Canada.

Joni Mitchell, "A Case of You"

I shan't have lied (Elizabeth Bishop, "One Art"): losing you was such a disaster that sometimes it's easier to forget that you still exist. But I don't forget for long. And as soon as I do, you all come back to me: like your waking after a winter's worth of sleep, your smile after the snow has mostly melted, your speaking the funny way you spoke.

It's evident (Bishop, "One Art"), what the Gospel sort of says: he who would gain his past shall first lose it.

Note: *Je me souviens* (official motto of Quebec).

5048. "hope"

> His unbelievable verdict is this hideous and upsetting world where even the moles dare to hope.
>
> Camus, "Appendix: Franz Kafka," *The Myth of Sisyphus*

Sometimes I feel like I'm just crawling along, fearful of something I can't see.

Right about then, I lose sight of all hope.

Now I wonder: are these forms of blindness brother and sister?

You see, it's not so much that I can't see any hope: it's more like I can't see much of anything to hope *for*. Those look different, don't they? One looks a lot like the end of a road, the other more like an open one.

People of our stripe have what sure looks like an infinite power to fear what we can't see. Maybe we have an infinite power to hope for what we can't see, too.

I hope so.

Note:

James Keller: Miss Sullivan? I'm James Keller.

Annie Sullivan: James? I had a brother Jimmy. Are you Helen's?

(W. Gibson, *The Miracle Worker*)

5049. "sure as tomorrow morning"

sure as tomorrow morning,
Amongst come-back-again things, things with a revival

Hopkins, "St. Winfred's Well"

Like the help that will heal the heart when it hurts: like the lightening that lightens before the light's letting in: like the *Send* of the sweetness that settles the sentence: you're like, *all that*, somehow.

Somehow, all that.

Note: “(who knows how)” (Hopkins, “Pied Beauty”).

5050. “a perfect edition of my works”

> I *must* make a perfect edition of my works, and then I shall have nothing to do but to die.
>
> Alexander Pope, “Conversations with Jonathan—I mean, *Joseph* Spence”

I think I’ll take a pass on this one. For one thing, I don’t want to die yet. And for another, I haven’t finished my works or my work and have no plans to retire anytime soon. How could I, what with all the new jobs coming in? Why, just this morning, a new assignment came down the pike—one of those *should you choose to accept it* deals. Did you know that at least according to one report, there are nonviolent bees in the Himalayas? ("I could not determine whether it was stingless, or just well behaved." – *The Asian Journals of Thomas Merton.*) Who would've guessed? Anyway, wouldn't it be great to be so mild, either through the offices of Nature or Culture?

I don't expect to lose my sting, but I'd sure like to learn how to soften its damage.

That shouldn't take too long: no longer than the rest of my life.

Note: "O grant me, thus to live, and thus to die!" (Pope, aka The Wasp of Twickenham, *Epistle to Dr Arbuthnot*).

5051. "full of pain"

who would lose,
Though full of pain, this intellectual being,
Those thoughts that wander through eternity.

Milton, *Paradise Lost*

I wonder why he says *Those* thoughts, rather than *these* thoughts?—the painful thoughts that awaken you in the night and feel like they'll stay forever.

Actually, though, they *don't* stay forever. They leave in the morning—or the morning after that—or, well, some morning after that. One way or another, they'll leave your allotted part of this intellectual being—just like everything else that dwells at the heart of the way we live here and now. (We were warned: don't get too used to anything, they told us. All that we think dear [dark or light] will pass out of our hands, someday. No thought we call our own really is: such properties prove themselves so many pilgrims, bound to wander toward a promised land beyond our own little plots, our own little sway.)

These thoughts—*those* thoughts: *look!* (Elizabeth Bishop, "One Art"): it's morning. They're already wandering away.

Note: "Wayfarers All" (Kenneth Grahame, *The Wind in the Willows*).

5052. Making It Through

There is no collapse of the will in Proust.

Samuel Beckett, *Proust*

Good to know, right? Talk about the *opposite* of helpful. At least so it seems that way at first (or at last). I mean, don't must of us feel our will collapsing and corroding at least a little every day?

It reminds me of what a friend said when we were driving through a blinding blizzard north of Montreal one terrible winter night, listening to Barry Manilow report to us on the radio how he'd *made it through the rain.*

“It doesn’t do the rest of us much good,” my friend observed.

On second thought, though, maybe the proud prospect of Proust’s indefatigable will offers more roadside assistance to the rest of us than the simple news of someone else’s triumph in the midst of our own turmoil. He got tired a lot, I understand, especially as he got older. We can all relate to that (especially after a night without sleep), so let’s just start there. It’s hard to be tired a lot, and scary. How can I possibly do what I know I have to do when I’m this tired? Sometimes

you get so damn run down, you wonder how you’re going to get to the end of the sentence or the session or the season you’re slated to finish.

But you do.

Note: “I can’t go on, I’ll go on” (Beckett, *Standard*).

5055. From Ritual to Romance

method … in the service of the self

Maurice Natanson, *Edmund Husserl: Philosopher of Infinite Tasks*

You're a creature of habit now. (Maybe you always were—"you've always been compulsive," my mother says—but you notice it a lot more now that you're alone so much with your daily routines.) You wake up first thing in the morning and make your bed. After that you—well, you fill in the rest.

On your good days, the track of your rituals leads to a weird little romance. Somewhere along its way, your method meets up with your madness, and each brings out the other one's personal best, the way that happy couples do. (You've seen it before.)

Your methods make your madness feel (for all its fear and trembling) a little at home in the world, like someone from a foreign country whose host teaches him enough of the language spoken there to get around.

Your madness, for its part, gives your method a little purpose in life.

And you know that the purpose is bigger than you.

Note: "Man … reveals and determines his situation by transcending it in order to objectify himself—by work, action, or gesture" (Sartre, "The Progressive-Regressive Method," *Search for a Method*).

5056. "pathless ways into happy ones"

> The first aim … is to show evidence of … perfect liberty … converting pathless ways into happy ones.
>
> Ruskin on the landscape of Dante's Paradise, *Modern Painters*, 3: xiii

On my first visit to his favorite foreign city, my best friend told me that to get to know a strange place, it was good to get lost a little there. Well, I got lost but good.

I got lost a lot that summer: It was the last time I got so lost.

It was the last time I fell in love.

Note: "unfettered and alive" (Joni Mitchell).

5057. Voir Dire

> He went on lying and telling stories until he became one of the world's great masters of the art, and created those grand imaginative lies which in our perplexed condition somehow approximate the truth.
>
> Steven Marcus, "Who Is Fagin?",
> *Dickens: From Pickwick to Dombey*

I don't worry about Dickens being hauled up on charges of Lying. Dickens knew his way around a courtroom, and he'd probably do a pretty good job representing himself (no fool, this Client). My guess is that he'd call only one witness—an expert character witness. Not that he'd listen to me, but I can tell you whom I'd have him bring in to testify. He's German and he's sort of dead and completely incompetent by now, but there would be no problem prepping his testimony: *Whosoever built a new Heaven has found the strength for it only in his own Hell* (Nietzsche).

"All those stories you told about people being better off and better than they could ever possibly be: how can you live with yourself?" the Prosecutor would ask.

Dickens would tell him off, big time: "Are you kidding? I only wish I could have told them taller!" he'd say.

He'd probably get off with Life.

And the Life that he'd save would be ours.

Note: "Tiny Tim, who did *not* die" (Dickens, "A Christmas Carol").

THE BIBLE
AUTHORIZED KING JAMES VERSIO
WITH APOCRYPHA
HOLY BIBLE
The OXFORD STUDY BI

DECEMBER 2013

5072. The Good Enough Beginning 269

The heavy and the weary weight
of all this unintelligible world
Is lighten'd.

Wordsworth, "Tintern Abbey"

It only needs to be lightened a little (enough to start a sentence or figure out a fear), and the next thing you know, even on a bad day, a frozen, foggy day, you've lessened your load enough to be on your way.

Note: "Affections gently lead us on" ("Tintern Abbey").

5074. "A Hundred Million Billion Sonnets"

December 5, 2013, at 8:35am

"A HUNDRED MILLION BILLION SONNETS"

Raymond Queneau, *OuLiPoetic*

All I need is one.
All it needs is you.

Note: "child of yours" (Shakespeare, "Sonnet 17").

5075. "He saw himself as a ludicrous figure"

> He saw himself as a ludicrous figure, acting as a pennyboy for his aunts, a nervous, well-meaning sentimentalist ... the pitiable fatuous fellow he had caught a glimpse of in the mirror.
>
> James Joyce, "The Dead"

Sometimes I see myself as a total fool and a total fake. I catch sight of myself in the midst of some caffeinated hyperbole—a programmed enthusiasm that a discerning viewer will quickly click past on the way to the higher channels—and I suddenly wish for a law against all kinds of mirrors. Sometimes my voice sounds so thin and eager that the only mercy I can imagine is a universal mute button.

In the midst of my wincing, though, I sometimes remember what a friend once observed when her infant son seemed drawn to me, as if I were a noisy and oversized mechanical toy: "Babies like Jeff. They like overacting."

For people like me, I guess, acting and overacting are sometimes hard to tell apart. And people like me just have to hope that babies aren't the only ones who can tell that.

Note:

> a man's reach should exceed his grasp,
> Or what's a heaven for?
> (Browning, "Andrea del Sarto")

5077. "like a tree of tears"

> Wonderstruck I sway, like a tree of tears.
>
> James Merrill, "Investiture at Cecconi's"

Struck, you remain rooted and ready to wonder, still. Stuck, you find yourself moving just the same. Sad as you seem, you still put out some shine.

After all, the perennials remain in one piece. Every sorrow has its seasons of light.

Note:

> great-rooted blossomer …
> body swayed …
> brightening glance …
> (Yeats, "Among School Children")

5079. Rage Comes Home to Root

the flash of recognition … as he whirled his stick upward

George Eliot, *Middlemarch*

The worst story, ever: some angry person from your past who knows everything bad about you finds out where you live now, and comes to destroy the peace that you've found since you got away from him. Wait, that's not the worst story ever. The worst story ever ends with the flash of recognition that he never left your side (*flesh of my flesh: Father, can't you see I'm burning?* – Genesis, Freud).

There's a better story after that, though. It's the one where you realize that you want to be on the side of sparing the rod (*terrible swift sword!*), not the side that rallies around it.

Note: "Blessed are the peacemakers" (Matthew 5:9).

5080. “if nobody can understand it?”

What’s the use of writing at all if nobody can understand it?

George Eliot, *Middlemarch*

Fair question. On the other hand, who would want to keep writing without at least a little mystery involved? It’s like the people you love. No matter how well you know them, you know there’s parts of them you’ll never really know. Sometimes, knowing you don’t know them shows how you love them.

Sometimes knowing you’re not knowing is the sign of what lasts.

Note:

December 11, 2013

Today I will give the last lecture in a course I teach on the nineteenth-century English novel. The lecture will take up *Middlemarch* one last time before everyone involved disperses to parts unknown.

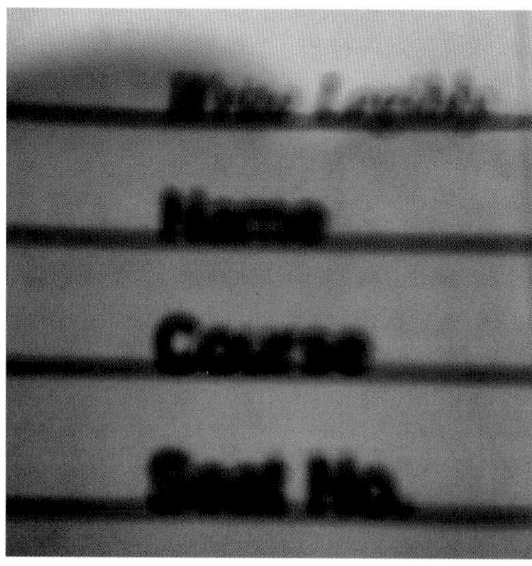

5086. "burning boy"

And love's the burning boy.

Elizabeth Bishop, "Casabianca"

He'll be waiting for you, that burning boy, way out at sea. He'll be waiting at least as long as it takes for you to find him. The deck he's on and everything else about him is also burning. He's been standing on that burning deck for a long time now, waiting for his father to relieve him of duty. (But his father's dead, so he can't.) You probably already know all this: the story's been repeated a lot. When you reach him, you can hear him tell it yourself, if you want. (He stammers a lot: I hope you'll be patient.) I think he'd like knowing that you want to hear him tell you the story he's been practicing so long to tell, even though you've heard it all before.

Actually, I think he'll love you for it.

Note: "faithful heart" (Felicia Dorothea Hemans, "Casabianca")

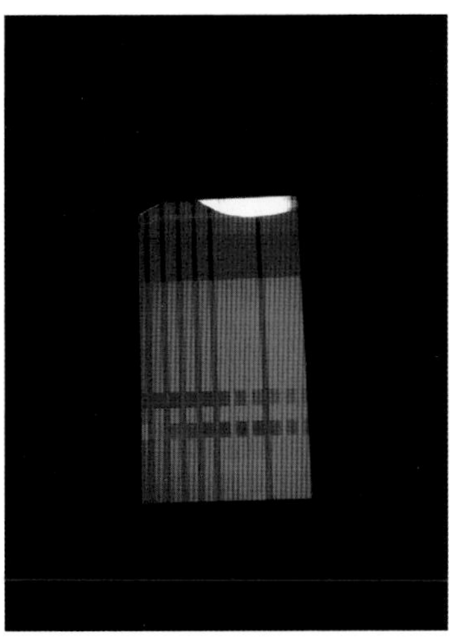

5092. "allies in the fight"

[*Emma*] proposes to us the hope of victory in the battle that the mind must wage, and it speaks of the expectation of allies in the fight.

Lionel Trilling, introduction to the Riverside edition of *Emma*

No one can fight your battles for you, of course. (Your parents taught you that, or should have.) On the other hand, if you've got good friends around, some of those battles can feel less like going to war and more like learning to love.

Note: "so dear to her" (Austen, *Emma*).

5093. Part for the Whole

All the communions of a life-time are one communion.

Teilhard de Chardin

Remember all those moments of truth you've had with others—all those times that you managed to bypass all the interference and really connect with the people around you?

You can't? Neither can I. Neither can anyone.

Sometimes you just have to count on the moments of closeness with others you *do* remember to stand for the ones that you don't.

Somehow, you hope that they can.

Note: "proposing frankly ... for those moments' sake" (Pater, conclusion to *The Renaissance*).

5094. News of the Day

> An angel, speaking to a group of shepherds in a field.
>
> Dickens, "A Christmas Tree"

A lot happens before and a lot happens after, but this has always been my favorite part of the story. Some migrant workers minding their own business somewhere out in the sticks suddenly hear from on high that a child's been born in a nearby city and that this birth is a matter of considerable importance to them, even though, technically speaking, they're not related.

Whatever special powers and promises may attach themselves to him, in one important way, he's just like every other kid: his birth is everybody's business.

Note:

> Each with his gift according to his kind
> Bringing this child his body and his mind.
> (Auden, *For the Time Being: A Christmas Oratorio*)

5095. "Somebody loves us all"

Elizabeth Bishop, "Filling Station"

Some days when you're not feeling lovable, you just have to take that on faith. (You've felt loved before. You'll feel loved again.)

It's like planning a road trip. You can't be absolutely sure that they'll be always be a gas station when you need it, but you don't let your uncertainty keep you at home.

All kinds of things have a funny way of turning up just in time.

Note: "able to approach the Future as a friend" (Auden for Freud).

5096. "real religious feeling"

Sometimes the Philosopher got so scared just sitting in his room that he didn't know how he would ever get out. He told a friend that when things got really bad, the only cure he knew was "religious feelings." The friend concurred:

> I replied that I didn't think that was crazy at all; that coming from Ireland I knew something of the power of religion. He seemed displeased with the answer as if I hadn't understood him.
>
> Wittgenstein: I'm not talking about superstition but about real religious feeling.
>
> And then we walked on in silence for some time. (M. O'C. Drury, "Conversations with Wittgenstein")

I think what the Philosopher meant by real religious feeling must have been what enters the room only after thoughts of power have left it. I guess it's what shows up when you care less about being the kind of person with Keys to open all kinds of doors, and more about being the kind of person kind enough to open up your own.

Note: "anxious in the right way" (Kierkegaard, *The Concept of Anxiety*).

5097. Seeing off People You Love

Tears of the widower, when he sees
A late-lost form

Tennyson, *In Memoriam*

December 28, 2013, at 7:36am

"I guess it's just weddings and funerals from here on in," my mother said a few years ago to someone she loves but doesn't see much anymore—never, in fact, except at weddings and funerals.

Maybe the mixing of weddings and funerals runs in the family. Lately, the only way I have to hold anyone comes when I see that he's basically already hit the road.

It takes all kinds of eyes to see the world.

Some of us can only have and hold the people we love when we see that they're good, or good enough, to go.

Sometimes we like to see how going and staying can feel too close to tell apart.

Note: "two eyes make one in sight" (Robert Frost, "Two Tramps in Mud Time").

5098. Old and New Friends

> How many in whose company I came into the world are gone already!
>
> Marcus Aurelius, *Meditations*

And I know it's just going to get worse and worse. (You should hear my mother on the subject.) Some of the ones who are gone (upstate now, or someplace further) were real beauties, by the way.

I miss them—though less so when I'm talking to the people I've met since the others left. Partly that's because I'm talking about the ones who have left and partly it's because I realize that I don't always have to.

Note: "the risk of being cured" (Sartre on "The Talking Cure" in *Being and Nothingness*).

5099. Lost and Found

> The incomplete or missing book is present in its fragments. It is not therefore absurd to imagine that, instead of a total book which would regroup all the combinations, it would be possible to write one of such insufficiency that the importance of what had been lost would shine forth from it.
>
> Pierre Macherey, "Borges and the Fictive Narrative," *A Theory of Literary Production*

Good to know. Good to know when you wake up in the morning—"it was exhausting just to be asleep," my best friend says—a little worse for being worn out by all those weird dreams about missing deadlines and documents. You have them, right? Can you send them my way if you're done with them? I need to put them together. It's the end of the year, and I have to start thinking about taxes. Wait, I just realized you can't give me what I need, since I'm not really sure what I need. I'll check back with you if I ever figure it out. (Don't hold your breath.)

Good to see that shining (see citation above) when you open your eyes in the morning, ready for real tears as those imaginary gardens filled with people you love have already mostly disappeared.

Those people you love: you were never really with them, not in any way you could ever say for sure. It was more like being with a book you read when you were really young, all about how as soon as you figure out what you're missing, you're halfway home to finding it. (At least you've got some kind of blueprint, that book said, though it may look like so many cracks on the surface of an empty bowl.)

You lost that book years ago. (Now you have someone else's copy.)

See? One way or another, coming or going (in circles, sometimes), what you've lost still finds a way to fill in your world.

Note: “Here something returns upon itself something coils around itself, and yet does not enclose itself, but frees itself in its very coils” (Heidegger, *The Essence of Reason*, qtd. by Macherey).

5100. "Now Voyager" (Whitman, H. Crane, C. Robinson)

Moby-Dick's dark, violent and enigmatic theme …

Newton Arvin, *Herman Melville*

Well, it's a good thing there are calmer mysteries than that particular dark-and-stormied dream.

There's that voyage from madness to mildness, for example, where a Captain of Anger, for no reason, starts to speak softly to a terror-crazed boy.

Then there's that Revelation (who knows from where?) that whatever it is you're trying to catch doesn't always have to be chased down to the bitter end.

Note: "lashings charmed and malice reconciled" (Hart Crane, "At Melville's Tomb").

JANUARY 2014

5102. Fool for Love

There are various orders of beauty, causing men to make fools of themselves in various styles *from the desperate to the sheepish* (George Eliot, *Adam Bede*), and no one has much say over the kind of ass he makes of himself for the kind of beauty he falls for—not much more than he does about the kind of beauty that lands him on his ass in the first place.

I hope you find admitting that to yourself as much a relief as I do.

Note: "touches my foolish heart" (Dorothy Fields, "The Way You Look Tonight").

5103. Keeping It Public

> For Johnson the highest virtues of style are the public virtues … keeping to what is central in human experience.
>
> William Edinger, *Samuel Johnson and Poetic Style*

You can drift away from the center, sometimes, just like you can forget to keep the promises you made. At least I can. Sometimes, the *need for speed* (T. Cruise, *Top Gun*), the need to feel all shining and new, acts like some strange storm system that keeps me dimly trapped in my old little room, far away from the places we share.

But then I remember that the only way I've ever dug my way through anything is when I've felt pretty sure that someone was waiting for me on the other side.

Through all kinds of weather, you just keep talking about all the things you share with other people and you just keep on burrowing through, till you reach the place where those others are there to meet you.

Note: "a companionable form" (Coleridge, "Frost at Midnight").

5104. "How can anyone want such things?"

Elizabeth Bishop, "Crusoe in England"

—all the things I used to need to make a life for myself on the desert island where I was stuck for so long.

(The local museum's asked me to
leave everything to them …)

I never even look at those things anymore. Why would I? Why would anyone else? I keep them in closets and file cabinets where no one has to see them. They're boring and dirty. I don't even know why I keep them around—old clippings and shoes now unfit for my print, or anyone else's. Then all those pictures I've kept—pictures of people I used to love when I was stranded. (Most the time, I don't even remember the person in the picture, much less who I was that I could love that person so.)

No souvenir helps me remember what really kept me alive during all those years alone.

I don't need a souvenir for that.

Note: "Friday, my dear Friday, died of measles seventeen years ago come March" ("Crusoe in England").

5105. Mint Car

Some set out with glorious equipment of hope and
enthusiasm … and get broken by the way.

George Eliot, *Middlemarch*

—actually, everything's at least a little broken, even before you drive it off the lot. (You find that out along the way.) And things break down and fall apart more and more as the mileage piles up. (That's just their way.) But if you can hold on to your ride long enough and keep the transmission tuned, you'll be driving vintage before you know it.

That's the Classic Way.

Note: "Long may you run" (Neil Young, "Long May You Run").

5106. Questions of Rescue

> One of the finest things men and women do is rescue men and women, even when they know they are rescuing the dead.
>
> Norman Maclean, *Young Men and Fire*

Sometimes, it takes basically no time at all, like when you help someone up from a slip. Other times, it takes a little longer, like when someone needs a line or a ladder. And then there are those times (like with the dead, sometimes) when it takes all the time in the world, and then some.

The thing is, you never really know beforehand how long it will take to help rescue someone, or what, if anything, *can* be rescued—what can be saved from fire or forgetting.

Still, though, it's pretty amazing how much work you can do in the dark.

Note: "As eagles eie, that can behold the sun" (Edmund Spenser, *The Faerie Queene*).

5111. "for One only"

> No artist lives and loves, that longs not Once,
> and only once, and for one only.
>
> Browning, "One Word More"

Only once? I guess it depends on what you mean by One. If One means a composite of Many (the whole collection of singles whom, at one time or another, you put above all others), well, count me in. I'm there. What I mean is, I'm *here*.

I'm here and I'm singing and *the song is you*.

Note: *E pluribus unum* (Standard).

5114. All for Love

Writing to you every morning: writing with all my might, and all my lack of it, has become very important to me. In fact, *these notes*, where *I make up my tunes for love* (Joni Mitchell, “For the Roses,” citation altered, but not by a lot), have become the most important part of my day.

So I just hate cutting short our morning call, whatever the more pressing demand (manuscripts, meetings) that obliges me to do so.

And now, look! I've spent as much time telling you how much I hate not spending time with you as on many a sunnier day I actually spend with you.

That's the heart of half the love poems ever written, right?

Note:

> Though these things as I ride be from mine eye,
> They're present yet unto my memory.
> (Donne, "Good-Friday, 1613, Riding Westward")

5118. I'm So Much Less Sure of Myself Now Than I Used to Be

As I look back on what I wrote a few years ago, what really stands out is how much more positive and prescriptive I seemed to have felt then than I do now. I am much less sure of myself and of everything about me now than I appeared to be then. That person who seemed so unfilled with doubt: I can't say I really remember him.

A lot of big doubts have crossed my threshold since. (Am I wrong about everything? Do I seem like an ass, just generally?) And then of course behind all that there is the doubt (my guess is that you know it too) that people have stopped loving me or will soon.

But I know that this feeling of doubt, close enough to dread that they are impossible to tell apart in the dark, will give way to the start of something fulfilling. I just know it. When? Soon enough. I know this as surely as I know that the sun will come up soon.

That's all for now. More later.

Note: "We don't remember as exactly the desperate moments when our lives are in the balance as we remember the moments after, when the balance has tipped in our favor and we know we are safe and have turned to helping others" (Norman Maclean, *Young Men and Fire*).

5119. "something understood"

George Herbert, "Prayer (I)"

Say you're sending a message to someone and you want it to be perfect. Say you're trying to reach someone you love as much as you remember ever loving anyone and you figure if you get what you have to say across just right (not too many words, not too few, not too big, not too small, and in exactly the right combination), you will. And when you do, it'll be like a magic carpet that'll take you straight to that other party's heart of gold.

So you keep weaving and reweaving your words until eventually you realize what you guessed from the start: What you most want to get through will get through as much despite your efforts as because of them.

What do you do then? You know: *Send.*

Note: "The soul in paraphrase, heart in pilgrimage" ("Prayer I").

The Human Part of Speech

5123. Notes as Novel

These notes, and the daily effort to connect collected in these notes, began partly as a joke—someone else's joke, actually: a big book of jokes and riddles called *Pale Fire*, by Vladimir Nabokov. It's an elaborate and sometimes hysterical ruse: a novel that pretends to be an annotated edition of a poem. The poem is called "Pale Fire." It consists of a thousand lines and is written by a fictional poet named John Shade. The notes for the poem are written by a fictional critic named Charles Kinbote, and they go on for several hundred pages. You get a pretty good sense of the poet, even though he's fairly quiet, and a pretty good sense of the critic, even though he talks all the time. It's an ingenious and very funny book, and it is also a book full of pain. The poet, a wry and oblique Robert Frost type, has a homely and lonely daughter who ends up taking her own life. (I guess she figures no one else would want it.) A lot of the poem seems to feel that loss. The critic, a crazy and fancy refugee, lost most the time in his own lost time, wants the poet and the poem to care most of all about that lost time. (It's the only way out.) But he doesn't and it doesn't, so the critic just goes about his narcissistic business, writing all these baroque and meandering notes that just pretend to explain various lines of the poem but are really all about his own private fears and fantasies. The book is full of pain, all right, the worst of which is that no one in it has any clue about the pain of anyone else.

The format of these notes (my notes) was born out of those notes (the novel's notes), and some of the notes that I first wrote sought to imitate their silly and supercilious self-centeredness. (Others went to the other extreme and don't mention me at all, seeking instead to be strict, sleek, self-effacing servants of the text standing over them for review.)

Lately, though, I've been thinking: wouldn't it be better for everyone concerned (artist and critic, daughter and father, writer and reader, lover and loved one, satire and sincerity, subject and object, past and present, before and after, young and old, living and dead, hunter and gatherer, prose and poem, player and pilgrim, pale and pregnant, parody and prayer) if we all just sort of met halfway and did our best to mingle with one another?

Everybody gets to be the star of the story if nobody has to be the only one.

Note: “Frankly I … never excelled in soccer” (note on line 130 297
of “Pale Fire,” *Pale Fire*).

Distressed Signal

5129. One Step at a Time

I been believing in nothing ever since I was born.

Flannery O'Connor, "Good Country People"

Meanwhile, I've been believing in something (finishing a sentence, getting through a cold, making a call on time). And I've been believing that you've been believing something like that, too.

Note: "that simple" (Flannery O'Connor, "Good Country People").

5130. Finding Your Way through Fear

"Was there not," Milner asks, "an *Odyssey* for those who were continually aware of their own weakness?"

David Russell, "Tact in Psychoanalysis: Paying Attention with Marion Milner"

I sure hope so. For some of us, admitting weakness looks like the only way back home. Every morning we wake up worried by what we see around us (burning towers, Cyclopses, men becoming beasts, greens about to turn yellow, etc.), and we wonder how we'll ever get there—home, I mean, or some other sure shore.

But maybe the fear itself somehow signals the path to such a shore (someplace beyond what we see when we're scared).

Maybe we can figure out how.

Note: “going gallant” (Hopkins, “The Leaden Echo and the Golden Echo”).

FEBRUARY 2014

300 **5134. Runaway**

> … constructed
> boxes where things hurry away from their names
>
> Octavio Paz, "Objects & Apparitions," trans. Elizabeth Bishop

They're not the only ones: sometimes when we're together in the little box of a condominium she calls home, my mother's up and gone somewhere else. (At such times, it feels a little like we're Mother-and-Son in name only—though so far, she's always made it back in time for dinner.)

She's hurried away to another room, or another part of this one, working puzzles on the computer or a little table. She says she does them to keep herself grounded, but I think she's partly checking flight schedules—plotting her next trip out of the box, or trying to put together what she'll see once she gets there.

I don't mind, though: one way or another, I know she'll find a way to write.

Note: "pilgrim soul" (Yeats, "When You Are Old").

My mom's always loved a coffee shop.

5137. Human Landscape

Walking in the winter can be awfully lonely. People naturally retreat into their own shells for protection. It helps to walk with a friend to ward off the loneliness a little. I had a friend who hated the winter as much as I do, and we used to walk a lot together in the cold. Neither of us thought we could stand it, alone. (We're both from warmer climates.)

One day my friend showed me a painting called *Green Sea* (maybe to take our minds off winter). It's a painting of two people walking along the beach. The landscape would look a lot less friendly without those two people walking on it, I thought. My friend went further. He believed you'd actually have some trouble figuring out it was a landscape at all, if it weren't for those people.

There are a lot of places that you wouldn't know were fit for human habitation if you didn't see people inhabiting them.

---

302 Note: "Turns them to shapes, and gives to airy nothing / A local habitation and a name" (Shakespeare, *A Midsummer Night's Dream*).

Milton Avery, *Green Sea* (1958)

5139. Interpretation of Dreams

The visions all are fled …
A sense of real things comes doubly strong,

… but I will strive
Against all doubtings …

Keats, "Sleep and Poetry"

I don't remember my dreams, and certainly wouldn't expect you to care to hear about them if I did. I have very little interest in the particulars of my own dreams and cannot imagine why anyone else would, either.

Besides, I think I have a pretty good idea of what they're all about. I think they're all about getting really close to other people and admitting how much you love them even when you say and feel that you hate them. (Your different feelings for other people get close to one another, too—the way enemies can end up admitting they want to be friends.) And the closeness doesn't stop there. It just keeps on going. The people you get close to in your dreams also get close to one another: so close that you can't really tell them apart. (It's sort of like how close I get to you: sometimes, I can't tell us apart.)

Closeness like that doesn't look like it could go on for very long—not much longer than the length of a dream. (Dreams seem to feel that their kind of closeness can't last. I think that's what often makes them sad.)

But I believe the closeness may last longer than the dreams that show such closeness appear to think it does. Closeness like that, once it gets started: who's to say where it ends?

Note: "a tremendous work of condensation" (Freud, "The Dream-Work," *The Interpretation of Dreams*).

minion over us? And they hated
him yet the more for his dreams,
and for his words.
9 ¶ And he dreamed yet another
dream, and told it his brethren,

Radical
Will

Noonday 536 $3.95

304

MARCH 2014

5191. How to Live 305

> The object of all art and learning is that we may know how to live.
>
> Ludovico Sforza, qtd. in Burkhardt,
> qtd. in E. M. Forster's *Commonplace Book*

—which is as good a reason as any I've ever heard to take up art and learning. I don't know about you, but just when I think I've got things figured out, something comes up and I get all confused again. (It's like what Bob Dole said, when he was running against Bill Clinton in 1996 and some reporter asked him what he thought the big issues of the campaign would be. "I don't know," he said. "Somethin'll pop up. Always does.")

He was right. (Bob Dole was right about a lot of things, in my view, but that's a whole other issue.) The point is that something *does* always come up that'll throw a wrench in your works—*a pageantry of fear* (Wordsworth, "Elegiac Stanzas Suggested by a Picture of Peele Castle in a Storm, Painted by Sir George Beaumont"), a knowing that you're gone, the feeling that you never will be, a love of the world that will never be enough to save it, the fact that my mother, no matter how much I write about her—anyway, you get the idea.

Now, where am I going with all this? Oh yes: a picture of Peele Castle or a picture of anything that reminds you of some calm and cool place that was once a big part of your life and that you come back to later only to realize that while it may have stayed the same, there was no way you could. What do you do with that? I'll tell you what you do with that. You try to get brave and calm and even a little happy with that (though you can see where it's trending—you're not an idiot):

> welcome fortitude, and patient cheer,
> And frequent sights of what is to be borne!
> (Wordsworth, "Elegiac Stanzas")

How do you do that? Well, you can start by looking again at the picture and realizing during your review session that most pictures which remind you of some peaceful, easy place from your past know that they're gone now (if they were ever there in the first place). Say, for example, it's a picture of some quiet beach:

> So pure the sky, so quiet was the air!
> So like, so very like, was day to day!
> (Wordsworth, "Elegiac Stanzas")

And then you notice that the picture reminding you of that beach is all beaten up by storms and scars and scares and sadness:

> This sea in anger, and that dismal shore.
> The lightning, the fierce wind, the trampling waves.
> (Wordsworth, "Elegiac Stanzas")

You feel less alone now, right? It turns out you're not the only one who sees something darker and different from a basic day at the beach—*So like, so very like, was day to day!* (Wordsworth, "Elegiac Stanzas"—God, I can still hear my Romantics professor reading that line out loud, softly but distinctly enough to reach across the distance of a lake or a decade full of dreams). So you've lost something. You lost someone—some peace, some person who meant peace. But look! Someone's here who's good with storms and sorrow.

He knew they were here before you did. Now, he's here to show you through.

Note: "lessons at love's pain and heartache school" (Jackson Browne).

APRIL 2014

308 **5211. Robert Frost**

> I would have to find a new way of looking at things I had known nearly all my life, such as scholarship and the woods.
>
> Norman Maclean, *Young Men and Fire*

When we were young, a friend and I used to make fun of Robert Frost. We thought his simplicity a sign of stupidity. (We are both academics, trained to esteem the conspicuously complex above all else.)

My friend and I no longer speak. As the years went on, we grew apart and fell out. I suppose it was inevitable, or maybe I just say that to myself because I just don't want to admit the possibility that it wasn't.

Anyway, I don't laugh at Robert Frost anymore, and while I cannot say for sure, my guess is that my friend doesn't either.

Note: "Nothing gold can stay" (Robert Frost, "Nothing Gold Can Stay").

MAY 2014

5236. Fantasy Fatherhood 309

> The … Struggle for Existence in a large and metaphorical sense, including dependence of one being on another, and including … not only the life of the individual, but success in leaving progeny.
>
> Darwin, *The Origin of Species*

I would have been a terrible father. The only kids I've ever hoped to have are those who would only be my kids when they felt like it. That's not fatherhood: that's fantasy. "When you get right down to it," as my mother likes to say, no one selects his inheritance (the color of the eyes, most contours of the I).

Speaking of fantasies and my mother, did I ever tell you how she used to read me all those stories about animal families when I was a child? They were all about different species living together and looking out for one another. There was usually one father figure amongst them whom no one was really afraid of—not really, anyway, not for very long.

The older animals would tell the younger animals about him—how he would come down hard on them if they got too far out of line. But I think the young ones usually saw through the fantasy pretty quickly. I think they only pretended to be scared and only for as long it suited them. I think they must have known that it was just a story the older ones felt like telling.

Note: "a base libel on Badger, who, though he cared little about Society was rather fond of children" (Kenneth Grahame, *The Wind in the Willows*).

5237. Love Story

> Things pass away, like a tale that is told.
>
> Dickens, *The Old Curiosity Shop*

And then all kinds come along to fill in for the things that have passed away. Some are so young that they've never heard your story before. Some are as old as the love that knows to pretend that it hasn't.

Note: "the storyteller … at home" (Walter Benjamin, "The Storyteller").

JUNE 2014

312 **5281. Then I Don't Feel So Bad**

For oft, when on my couch I lie
In vacant or in pensive mood,
They flash upon that inward eye
Which is the bliss of solitude;
And then my heart with pleasure fills,
And dances with the daffodils.

Wordsworth, "I Wandered Lonely as a Cloud"

You know those days when all you want to do is to lie on the couch and make it go away—you're not even really sure what it is, you just know that it makes you too tired to do anything but lie on that couch. (It doesn't even bring you to tears, although things seem like they're headed that way.) All you can think about is how all you can think about is lying on that couch and dreading the next time you have to be around anyone else. So there you are, lying on that couch, and suddenly the sound of some stupid pretty song or the sight of some stupid pretty scene will pass your way as if it's come for you. And then you think maybe it really *has* come for you—only not just you: it's come for everyone else on that couch, too. (It's a big couch, though you only see your own small section of it.) You suddenly know in a flash they're not as stupid as they seem. (For one thing, they know how we're sad.) And once you know they're not stupid, you know you can take it from there.

Press Play.

Note: "And then I don't feel so bad" (Oscar Hammerstein, "My Favorite Things").

JULY 2014

314 **5290. Revelation Roulette**

Love's the boy stood on the burning deck
trying to recite "The boy stood on
the burning deck." Love's the son
stood stammering elocution
while the poor ship in flames went down.

Love's the obstinate boy, the ship,
even the swimming sailors, who
would like a schoolroom platform, too,
or an excuse to stay
on deck. And love's the burning boy.

Elizabeth Bishop, "Casabianca"

It's the sudden-death round now, and it's your turn to talk (one of those now-or-never situations), and naturally you want to make sure you cover everything you've learned. (You better—it's your only shot: it's like what my sister said about the high-stakes soccer game we watched the other day: "Jeff, now it's not win or go home, it's win or *don't* go home"—only now there's really no winning and no going home (not like you used to, anyway)—not with the ship going up in flames and you and everyone else down to the bottom of the sea: no winning and no going home, just standing and delivering and putting your all into saying something, some way, you hope someone, someday will call, will call—wait, before I forget: did I just say now or never? That was a slip of the tongue. Sorry: I stumble a lot in clutch situations: I meant now *and* never.

Anyway, where was I? Oh yeah, with you and me (and everyone else in between), and things don't look so good, but you're gonna give everything you got. So, there you are, out there on that limb of a deck: you're a student, you're a son (you hope good ones), maybe even a teacher, too—maybe everything under the sun, maybe some part of every son—and sister, too.

So there you are, out on that limb trying to show that you
know all the lines and all the lines of everyone before you. That's the hope, anyway. (*Luck be a Lady Tonight*, right?)

> The dice of drowned men's bones he saw bequeath
> An embassy.
> (Hart Crane, "At Melville's Tomb")

You're not exactly feeling the hope in the words, yourself, though, what with everything on fire and underwater, or about to be, you included. Still, though, that's the hope anyway: that along with the spreading of burning and drowning, something else spreads, too—something, some way, someone, someday will call, *will call, will call* (*Write* it!) Love.

Notes:

1. "world without end" (Ephesians 3:21).
2. *Write* it! (E. Bishop, "One Art").

Look carefully, and you'll see what's left of that boy (see above) in these clouds. Of course, if you look carefully, you'll see what's left of him everywhere.

5213. Why We Teach

> The effect of her being on those around
> her was incalculably diffusive.
>
> George Eliot, *Middlemarch*

You're getting older and you feel it: more listless, maybe lazy, more longing for some end. Still, though, on your good days, you can still teach your heart out. ("If you're not going to do the job right, there's no point in doing it at all," many a mother used to say.) You like to see people doing the best they can with what they have, and you like to think that part of what they have is all that you have to give them.

Note: "these actions of the sun" (James Merrill, "Cloud Country").

11 BEST BETS THAT BLEW IT
World Cup
TIME
LEGENDARY TEAMS

5218. Good Enough for Good-bye

lights a lovely mile

Gerard Manley Hopkins, "Poem 47"

Wouldn't it be great if we could come up with words fit to be the last thing we say to the people and places we love? They wouldn't have to be fancy, those last words, all dressed up. They wouldn't have to be words fine enough to finish a novel: more like words good enough to start one.

Note: "Miss Brooke had that kind of beauty which seems to be thrown into relief by poor dress" (George Eliot, *Middlemarch*).

INDEX

Numbers in italic indicate an illustration. Names in italic indicate fictional characters.